M000236191

I'm Leaving you for a White Woman

by

Mickey Royal

ENJOY *Mickey Royal*

Mickey Royal

I'm Leaving you for a White Woman
Published by Sharif Publishing

Library of Congress Cataloging-in-
Publication Data is available upon request.

Manufactured in The United States of
America.

Cover design by Olaf Donkers, Europe

I'm Leaving You For A White Woman

Dedication

This book is dedicated to;
My late great Mentor
Leslie Mohammed, Baba the Great
Elephant. I love and miss you…..everyday.
.

Mickey Royal

Based on a true story

TABLE OF CONTENTS

Mickey Royal

Chapter 1

As spring went away and made room for a long hot summer. Dennis knew his life would soon be drastically different. Having graduated with a 3.1 grade point average his dream of playing professional basketball flew away like the free throws he never hit. Not much of a point guard in college. Having been a star athlete in high school, shattering previous records, Dennis didn't quite measure up in college.

On a college level the competition was compiled of the best high school players in the nation. But being a 4.0 student in high school plus a 3.1 college student Dennis was a perfect selection for his current position as athletic coordination at his old high school. He was hired on the spot. There was no confusion as to whom the school wanted. Dennis wore several different hats at Central High School his Alma Mater.

Dennis taught 11th grade English, as well as athletic coordinator. His first day of the job Dennis found out that athletic coordinator was merely a fancy word for P.E. Teacher. His disappointment conflicted with his gratitude. Central High School felt honored to have the man who holds so many school records working at the school.

Dennis's classroom was decorated with the late greats of the Los Angeles Lakers. As a first-year teacher he wasn't as comfortable in his classroom as he was on the P.E. field. Although comfortable, being back where he once was a king amongst men was bittersweet. But Dennis was up for the challenge.

The first day on the job started as most of his days started. 5:00 a.m. Dennis begins his day unlike most bachelors with a half-mile jog around the neighborhood. He returns at 6:00 a.m. for a protein shake and a shower before heading to work. Dennis prefers to arrive early.

As he was setting up his room, students began to enter the room. Dennis was an adequate English Teacher, but he excelled on the P.E. field. As month after month passed by, he grew more and more into his new job and the required tasks.

Like clockwork every Saturday Dennis would visit his mother. He kept a copy of her key on his keyring. Whether his mother was home or not Dennis would arrive without calling. He would let himself in and begin doing chores. He would start in the kitchen by washing dishes, taking out the trash then sweeping and mopping the floor. His mother would always wait until she smelled the strong odor of Pine Sol before entering the kitchen.

"Catherine is that you?" his mother yelled.

"No mom, you know who it is!" answered Dennis.

Even though he knew the question was rhetorical he answered his mother with a disapproved sigh.

"Oh, I thought it may have been Cathy. She just left with the baby. You just missed her."

"No mom I didn't just miss her. We're not exactly each other favorite people, but I haven't seen Princess in a week" answered Dennis.

Dennis's mother knew that mentioning Catherine and Princess would touch a nerve in her son. That was his mother's way of obtaining information about Dennis's 8-year-old daughter Princess or her mother Catherine.

Dennis and Catherine were never married. They met in high school and attended the prom together. Dennis's mother so wanted grandchildren she made every effort to get them to the alter. Although they never married, Dennis and Catherine did have a daughter while in college. A beautiful little girl named Princess Alexander.

"What did Cathy say?" asked Dennis.

"She didn't mention you, she just brought the baby by."

Dennis and his mother were discussing marriage while Dennis was washing her dishes. Dennis's parents were happily married until the sudden death of his father two years ago.

Dennis's father died suddenly from a massive heat attack brought on by decades of cigarette smoking. After his death, Dennis's mom developed empty nest syndrome at the same spiraling into a deep depression. She became bitterly cynical using guilt to manipulate her son's life. Even though Dennis knew this, his mother was usually able to push his buttons.

Dennis finished the dishes and sat on the couch to engage in a full conversation about his love life.

"Son, you know I'm just worried about you. Cathy looks real pretty" his mom said.

"Mom, her looks were never the problem" Dennis snipingly answered.

"I just want Princess to have the best. Mom we're Co-parenting, just leave it alone."

Dennis got up to head to the gym.

"Bring me some Bar-B-Q."

"Mom, I'm going gym."

As Dennis looked back, he saw the overt look of disappointment on her face. Then he said "Okay." Dennis's mom knew how to pull his strings and push his buttons. But of course she would, she installed them. Dennis's love for his mother Florence was evident.

He primarily pitied her for using guilt as a weapon which made her a permanent victim in his eyes. For the sake of his mother, Dennis had agreed to go to counseling months ago. He couldn't ever refuse her once she turned on the faucet of passive aggressive guilt. Dennis had once tried couples counseling with Catharine to no avail. After only 3 sessions the arbitrary counseling evolved into full blown arguments. Both participated in the minimizing, denial and blame game. At such point the therapist strongly suggested individual counseling. Catherine first agreed then later un-provokingly changed her mind, after only attending two sessions.

Dennis however was a different animal all together. He took this opportunity not just to vent but to soul search. He figured why not. He was at the end of his rope. Dennis had an appointment for Friday for one hour. He couldn't understand why he was labeled the bad guy by his sister, aunt and even his mother.

He was convinced he had done right. He was desperate. More than anything he wanted the women in his family to be on his side. Dennis lived with the guilt of his father after his father's death. He had no one to turn to until he began counseling sessions. Without participation from his daughter's mom Catherine, Dennis decided to be totally honest.

Mickey Royal

Chapter 2

Dennis was nervous his first day of counseling. He felt weird being there by himself. He knew he needed therapy, and someone not connected to him personally to hear his story. He was looking for confirmation of his sanity. Besides, if it could lead to a better relationship with his daughter's mom and possibly seeing his daughter on a consistent basis, he was willing to try anything.

As he got comfortable on the couch he began to relax, and talk. His doctor Sylvia was a middle-aged woman of east-Indian decent. She was firm, but gentile. As Dennis began to speak about the relationship between he and Catherine she stopped him.

"Tell me about your previous relationship."

Dennis began to become noticeably uncomfortable as he was asked to recall Ruby. He had all but blocked the memory of her out of his mind. It took a few minutes, but Dennis began to open up about Ruby.

Ruby was a gorgeous woman. She was equally as smart as she was elegant. You could honesty instantly tell. Dennis was immediately attracted to her. She was 12 years older than him, but you couldn't tell by looking at her. She was caramel completion with shoulder length hair.

Ruby had a smile so warm it could melt the polar caps. Dennis met Ruby at the 24^{hr} gym one night. He was immediately captivated. Not only by her beauty but her witty repartee. She was quick with the puns that seemed to roll off her tongue with rehearsed ease. At the time of there meeting, Ruby was involved in a conversation in the sauna with three men simultaneously. Although outnumbered, she held her own in the lightweight debate.

Dennis felt he had a decent chance with her, in his mind Ruby was giving him the eye. He was fantasizing about being with her sexually while she was speaking. During his fantasy his ears went deaf. When she asked him a question his mind drew a blank. He responded with the usual male "uhm" that she was far too familiar with.

Ruby knew how visually stunning she looked. She also knew her worth as a successful black professional woman in her 40's. Dennis wanted to make his move when the sauna cleared out. He was far too attracted to her to let her get away. She intrigued him. Before the night ended, they both ended up in the hot tub. All of Dennis's hunches were right. Ruby was attracted to Dennis immediately. Ruby was the type of woman men wanted to marry.

I'm Leaving You For A White Woman

She had been married twice before. She was extremely articulate when she spoke. Intelligence exited her mouth as she chose her words carefully. Ruby had it all together from the outside looking in. They exchanged numbers and began dating a few days later.

The first date totally threw Dennis off. Ruby met Dennis sitting down in the sauna at the gym. Then they later met up in the hot tub. In the water is where their numbers were exchanged. Their first in person date was the first time they looked at each other standing up.

Dennis arrived at her house ten minutes early. He was as well dressed as he was anxious. This was the first time he'd dated an older woman. When Ruby opened the door, the first thing she said was "Wow, short but cute." Then she kissed him and stepped on the porch closing the front door behind her. Ruby was smiling all the way to the car. She offered to drive. Dennis agreed since he had driven so far to meet her. Ruby lived about an hour outside of the city.

They went to breakfast. Ruby took it upon herself to order for the both of them. Because of Ruby's age, Dennis allowed Ruby certain liberty's he wouldn't have allowed a woman closer to his age. He could barely think straight from the loud sound of his own blood rushing from his brain to his manhood.

Ruby wanted to take it slow with Dennis. Dennis was also cautious. But neither of them could deny how they obviously both felt. On the way back to Ruby's house Dennis began rubbing Ruby's leg.

Ruby made no comment neither did she move his hand. In fact, Ruby suggested he spend the night one day. Dennis decided that day would be today. Ruby assumed she and Dennis would get together some time that week.

Dennis was adamant about coming back that day to spend the night. Ruby laughed assuming Dennis was joking. She figured this was Dennis way of saying that he was attracted to her. She said to herself "He's bluffing." Although the thought of a younger man being so attracted to her validated her in a small way.

Dennis drove all the way home alone. He was so excited, he didn't want to make a mistake. He was as nervous as he was excited. He packed an overnight bag with toothbrush and headed right back out. He knew he had an hour drive in front of him, so he settled in for a long drive. He drove to her right in the middle of rush hour traffic. The one-hour drive took close to two hours. By the time he arrived it was dark. He didn't want to take any chances.

Dennis had popped a virga and a Nodose alone the way. He was positive he wanted to make a great impression. Dennis knew a woman 12 years his senior has probably had more sex than him thus sexual partners. Because of his age and the age gap between the two of them, Dennis felt he represented younger men around the world.

When he knocked on the door Ruby started laughing. She thought he was bluffing. She had no choice but to let him in, she was quietly happy Dennis came back the same day/night.

I'm Leaving You For A White Woman

Ruby welcomed him inside her home. She was on her way to becoming a real estate mogul. She was elegant from head to toe. Dennis felt he and struck gold. Ruby had prepared a dinner for the two of them that was to die for. She had a thing for one glass of cranberry juice every night. After dinner, Ruby poured the them both a glass of cranberry juice mixed with a dry champagne. As they walked up the stairs Dennis was reserved. As soon as the two of them hit the bedroom, Ruby turned on the T.V. and went to take a shower. She kept the door open so she could speak to him while she showered. She came out of the shower dressed in white lingerie. If there was any doubt in his mind about her intensions, all doubt was removed at first glance of her attire.

Dennis went to take his shower while Ruby set the mood with music from her era and scented candles. Dennis emerged from the bathroom in his night clothes. The two of them embraced in a kiss which lead to a weekend of incredible sex. The first night went down in history called Dennis's life.

Dennis was 28 at the time and Ruby was 40. It's a proven fact that women reach their sexual peak in there 40's. It's also proven that men reach theirs in their 20's. When those two peaks combine there's nothing short of an instant inferno. 'Mentally, Dennis had moved in with Ruby after the first night he entered her. Surprisingly Ruby was all for it. After the first two weeks she started to suggest it. Dennis also felt it made perfect sense since he was seeing Ruby every night. The drive, the gas, meant nothing to him, he was driving to

Ruby's every night. When he'd spend a night, he would have to leave her house at 5:30 a.m. just to get to work on time. So, after only 90 days of dating, Dennis gave his landlord a 30-day notice.

Over the course of the 30 days, Dennis slowly but surely moved his belongings to Ruby's house. Most of Dennis's personal belongings ended up in storage. There wasn't enough room for his things. Ruby's home was already well furnished. This didn't seem to bother Dennis at all. This was only the second time that Dennis had lived with a woman.

He and Catherine had moved into a place together when Catherine was pregnant with their daughter Princess Alexander. Dennis and Cathy were engaged at the time though they never married. The first two months went exactly as Dennis had hoped. He had developed such a love for Ruby that he actually fell in love with her. Even his co-workers got a mouthful from Dennis about his older new flame.

Dennis's mother and Ruby initially didn't get along. That was because Dennis failed to mention the age gap. Dennis kept that part to himself on purpose. He wasn't scared of her disapproval as much as he was her insults. He knew with his mother's pessimistic attitude and Ruby's sharp wit, it could lead to a show down of savage proportions.

Dennis mother Florence was known to run off a great number of Dennis's previous girlfriends. Dennis vowed to himself he wasn't going to let anything, or anyone come between him and his new mature bombshell. Ruby was very particular. She knew exactly what she wanted, when and how. If anything, or anyone exercised free will and ventured outside of her predisposition of what she viewed as right would result in immediate conflict. Before long, Dennis felt he was living in Ruby-land. Even though Ruby appeared to be running the show, Dennis was on cloud nine. The relationship at this point was still in its embryonic stage. More commonly known as The Honeymoon Stage. Ruby had a flair for decorating that Dennis appreciated. During the next three months at the six-month mark, Ruby and Dennis were becoming use to each other. They made love 2 to 3 times a week. Ruby was always the one who initiated it.

Once he heard his sister say in reference to Ruby "You can't handle a strong black woman." The response posed yet another question "Why does she require handling? Is she not human? She's not some wild circus animal." What did she mean when she said "Handle?" Was she referring to handle as in control? Control is impossible without complete submission. Submission requires permission from the will of the one who is submitting. Control without permission is subjugation, not submission.

The will of Ruby would never submit. Because her perception of submission is synonymous with defeat. Defeat is a word which implies loss by conflict. In order for there to be a defeat, there must be a contest of two or more opposing forces. Ruby felt that there is was conflict. A battle for control in relationships.

In any battle there will be causalities as well as collateral damage. The level of casualties and collateral damage depends on the velocity of the two opposing forces in question. Thus, making compromise virtually impossible.

Over time Dennis began to feel he must win to save his own individuality. His manhood came into question, asked by Dennis, to Dennis. Thus, the seed of self-loathing had been planted in the soil of his soul. As these feelings festered and began to take root in the field of time, the seeds would crosspollinate into insecurity, cynicism, anger, stress, which would display itself in a passive aggressive manner.

Dennis found himself actually competing against Ruby for the steering wheel in the car of their relationship. Both Dennis and Ruby found themselves in competition, not cooperation, a tumultuous tug of war. Before a wall breaks, it first will crack. Cracks in a wall are unpredictable. You have no control where or how the crack cracks. Usually it's not split evenly. And rarely, a crack does not splinter.

Depending on the degree of pressure from the opposing forces which determines the cracks. If the conflict causes a crack called insecurity, the crack of insecurity can splinter into infidelity, anger, resentment. Up to and non-excluding domestic violence. To avoid conflict, Dennis took the least line of resistance and submitted to the will of Ruby. Such a course of action turned Dennis into the Beta Male. From the outside looking in Dennis appeared to be "whipped."

I'm Leaving You For A White Woman

Truth is, he had become emasculated. In some cases, he would be perceived as weak. Rendering him neutered and non-effective. At that point, cracks have splintered, causing an actual redesigning of the very brick itself. The crackles unbroken brick is synonymous with the relationship. A oneness, firm complete and strong. But there are many elements that make up this rock-solid structure.

Ruby used many weapons at her disposal. She's armed with higher earnings and a quick condescending wit. Any chance to lash Dennis with her razor-sharp tongue in public, she exploited. She saw herself in such opposition to Dennis that when breaking him down she actually grew stronger in her mind. In a kind of an emotional S and M exchange verbally delivered. This rendered Dennis passively speechless.

Leaving him with one of two choices; 1) challenging her or 2) adapt into a beta male. Ruby's subconscious mission was to emasculate Dennis. Since she confused any display of masculinity with aggression. This warped view justified to herself her constant chip on the shoulder attitude. Since Ruby didn't have a relationship with her father, she felt personally attacked when dealing with an alpha-male.

For the sake of peace, Dennis knowingly participated in his own emasculation. In order for Ruby to feel comfortable, she had to be in constant and complete control. Controlling him with her finances was her main weapon. This immediately neutralized any hope of him ever being the dominant one in their relationship. In the beginning, Ruby showered Dennis with gifts. This was because Ruby felt when you love someone, you do all you can to please them. That was the position taken by her conscious mind. Her subconscious mind however had a sinister side. In order for Ruby to feel safe, she must be in control. Her lack of faith in her men stimmed from her subconscious disdain for the opposite sex.

In Ruby's mind, Dennis was a good man. She often referenced him in discussions with her girlfriends. Whenever he does anything that she deems as "not right" she used the excuse "He's just being a man." Over time, as this situation developed, Dennis became more and more complacent.

He enjoyed the lifestyle their combined income provided. But it came at the price of his self-esteem and masculine identity. Since he moved into her home, every time she got angry, she'd present the ultimatum; "My way or the highway." The need to control came from a deep-rooted fear. Lack of confidence in Dennis became to create a crack which splintered into anxiety.

Ruby defined herself by the amount of money she made. She also defined the world around her by the same standard. Ruby had been totally raised by her mother. Her examples of manhood came from two places. 1) Television 2) Her past failed relationships. Ruby's example of how a woman talks to a man were based on how her mother spoke to Ruby's brothers. Ruby grew up with her two brothers.

I'm Leaving You For A White Woman

Their mother was the matriarch and sole provider in the family. Ruby was the middle child of a single parent. Her mother worked hard and proudly boasted about her two college educated children, Ruby and her baby brother Ronald. The classic single mother; over worked, underpaid unfulfilled. Her parental philosophy steaming from the pain of rejection. Because Ruby's mom was a single parent, there were no contrary opinions in that home. No democracy, just a totalitarian dictatorship. What mother said was law. She was forced to be mom and dad.

In a two-parent home the burden of responsibility is shared. A scale must have an equal weight on both sides in order to maintain balance. But when there's one parent, the children have no other adult present to appeal to when a punishment or decision is handed down. That leaves no situation able to be challenged.

The oldest child, Ruby's brother Raymond, grew up with a chip on his shoulder. As the oldest male he felt like the man of the house. Whenever he attempted to flex his testosterone, it was quickly defeated by his mother's aggressive estrogen. Subconsciously Raymond felt his mother was the number one enemy of his evolution from boy to man. This situation developed a crack. What was left was a rebellious man-boy.

By the time Raymond was 18, he had gone to jail on numerous occasions. He grew up and lived his life in constant need of his mother's approval. But Ruby's younger brother was quite opposite.

Ronald being the baby had a different relationship with his mother. At the time of Ruby's parents' divorce, Raymond was 12. He and his father were close prior until Raymond's father was removed from his life far too soon. He had begun his journey into manhood guided by his father. Once his testicular navigational guide was gone, it left Raymond to continue the journey in the opposite direction lead by his mother.

Ruby's younger brother Ronald was a baby at the time of their divorce. Ronald became a conformist. Being a carbon copy of his mother, his characteristics mimicked that of a female. He was emotional and oft times quite defensive. Having only her mother as an example, Ruby inner acted with Dennis in the same manner as her mother dealt with her sons.

During time of conflict, when confronted with an issue, Ruby was known for verbally aggressive outbursts etc. "You are not my father!" or "Who the hell do you think you are!" Needless to say, Dennis and Ruby didn't last. Ruby could never internalize and analyze her part in why the relationship met with such an abrupt end. Ruby honestly felt she did everything wrong. She loved Dennis the way she learned from her mother. Ruby's mother worked a fulltime and part-time job.

Her mom dealt with Ruby's grown brothers the same way Ruby dealt with Dennis. All the wild not realizing that Ronald and Raymond were her mother's sons (children) not her mate. Ruby never was able to confront the issue of the sudden absence of her father.

I'm Leaving You For A White Woman

Ruby was 8 years old when her parents divorced. Her anger stimmed from the divorce she couldn't even acknowledge. Confronting the fact that she had become a stereotype and was part and partially responsible for the collapse of her and Dennis' relationship was inconceivable.

Since Ruby's perception of men was warped, then her views about men were distorted. How does one expect to find treasure when the treasure map is charted incorrectly? That voyage would be long and result-less. Ruby believed in order to have the perfect man she had to build him. Doing this by destroying what he knows and replacing it with what she wants him to know. This stemming from her fear of the unknown and anxiety she felt when confronted with her belief system of relationships.

When Dennis would bring up her short comings, Ruby would answer the question with a financial answer. As time went on, Ruby and Dennis's relationship evolved into a stagnant friendship at best. Dennis moved out and into his own place closer to his job. Their once physical relationship turned into a once a week phone call at best. Both equally deciding to go their separate ways.

Mickey Royal

Chapter 3

Dennis's counselling sessions were going fine. He had many of them left to complete. So, he decided that it was in his best interest to continue to be as honest and open as possible. In order to do this, Dennis would have to face the man in the mirror, and no matter how you sneak up on a mirror it always looks you right in the eyes. He was eager and determined to get to the root of his problem.

Catherine had not been to any of his sessions. She may have served as a distraction anyway. How honest could he be with her present. In the beginning, Dennis was happy to go to work and resented the counselling sessions. After a major breakthrough, Dennis began to look forward to the sessions. He was curious to know what the outcome would be. With each session, Dennis grew more eager.

But the sessions also left him completely drained. After every counseling session he'd go home and straight to sleep.

The Ruby recollective stories however didn't seem to effect Dennis. He had bigger fish to fry. Catherine Peterson, the mother of Dennis's 8-year-old daughter had him served with child support papers.

He was served one morning while having breakfast with his mom, Florence Alexander. The doorbell rang and Dennis answered the door only to come face to face with a process server. Dennis kept calm as his mother was badgering him about who it was. Dennis sat down and seemed to have lost his appetite. He showed his mom the papers, but his mom wasn't shocked. She had actually been expecting them.

Catherine knew that Dennis had breakfast with his mother every Saturday. Florence had actually taken Catherine several days prior downtown to file the papers. Just then, Dennis remembered when he called his mom Thursday that they were together.

Instantly Dennis got a bad taste in his mouth. He finished breakfast silently and left without saying a word. Since Dennis's mother lived alone, she had built a secret mother and daughter relationship with Catherine. Florence figured that if Dennis and Catherine fought in or out of court that Catherine might limit Florence's access with her daughter Princess.

Florence as a rejected bitter black woman saw kinship in Catherine. Catherine however didn't feel the same way. Catherine just used Florence for free babysitting and financial favors. The favors never went the other way.

Dennis resented how easily his mother threw him under the bus for a chance at getting on Catherine's "good side." Dennis felt irreversibly betrayed by his own mother. Catherine had driven a permanent wedge in the mother and son relationship they one shared. Florence seemed comfortable basking in the bitter pathetic pool of self-pity. Florence played the victim, and in her vulnerable state, Catherine took advantage of that.

Dennis had no relationship whatsoever with Catherine's mother or any of her family members. Catherine's was extremely vindictive and sinister in her methods. The court date was set for next month. Dennis entire mood had changed. On his way home he decided to go by the gym. It was open 24 hours and it had become his sanctuary. He kept his iPod on him for such and emergency. He would work out his stress on the treadmill. Dennis also kept a bowling ball and a gym bag in the trunk of his car.

Dennis couldn't help thinking that when he had moved in with Ruby sparked Catherine's latest attempt at maliciously disrupting the peace in his life. As he arrived at the gym, Ruby was on his mind. This is where they first met. He knew in the back of his mind Ruby wasn't there. Ruby only went late at night. Dennis did an hour on the treadmill then headed to the steam room and sauna.

The gym was pretty empty on the weekends. Dennis stayed at the gym for an hour then drove home. He had lesson plans to prepare for Monday. His once romantically filled Saturday nights he now spent alone. Dennis enjoyed two things, the gym and his therapy sessions.

Dennis did all he could not to let the pain of his mother's relationship with Catherine upset him.

At work Monday morning it was apparent that Dennis had something troubling on his mind. His students as well as his co-workers could tell. Dennis was in night school twice a week. He was studying to get his master's degree. He had a lot on his plate. To calm his nerves, he would call his favorite uncle. His uncle had been through it all when it came to women. His heart had been used as a hockey puck a few times.

Dennis was forced to take an honest look in the mirror. To find the victory in his future he first had to look at the defeats of his past, honestly. Dennis had come to his Monday night session and was surprised to see it was a group session. It bothered Dennis a little, but he figured he'd go with the flow.

Dennis remembered Keisha. Dennis met Keisha at the supermarket. The warning signs were everywhere but Dennis couldn't read them. Maybe because he was blinded by the butt on this woman. She was an attractive dark complexed woman in line in front of him. She stood about 5'1" with a large butt and a small waist. Dennis was so caught up in how she looked he failed to pay attention to what Keisha was saying on her cell phone.

As Dennis parked his basket behind Keisha, she was in a heated argument with the cashier. Keisha was in full ghetto mode right down to the eye and neck rolling stereotype. Below the belt insults seemed to come out of Keisha's mouth as if they were scripted.

I'm Leaving You For A White Woman

Keisha appeared to be in the zone. As if she was dancing to music. She told her story with her right hand and fluttering fingers resembling a bird flapping its wings. The veins in her neck got thicker appearing more vascular. She possessed the mouth of a sailor, the wardrobe of a prostitute with the volume of a bullhorn. All Dennis could see was her body and her side profile while she spoke. Apparently, Keisha was having some sort of dispute about the price of a scanned item.

The cashier was as polite as he could be. He was so intimidated by her obnoxious behavior that it rendered him speechless. He finally ended up summonsing the manager to speak to her. As if she was speaking another language and needed and interpreter. When the manager arrived, she held up her hands in a surrendering posture. The manager literally tip toed up to the checkout counter to attempt to solve the problem. The manager finally just unscanned the item and gave it to Keisha for free. Both the cashier and the manager appeared petrified as if they were cornered by a wild animal or savage beast.

Keisha left the store apparently still upset because she kept cursing out loud with no one in front of her. Keisha pushed her full basket as Dennis came running behind her. He caught up with her as she got to the trunk of her car. Keisha stopped short after loading just one bag when she noticed Dennis. Keisha immediately took a defensive posture. Before she could utter a word, Dennis spoke. Dennis could tell Keisha was still angry over the grocery store exchange.

So, he approached with extreme caution. Dennis was wearing his trademark ear to ear smile. He immediately offered his assistance with her groceries and began to show his support for her side over the cashier. After a brief conversation, Keisha tore off a piece of her grocery bag and wrote down her phone number for Dennis. Dennis was leading to that inevitable question, but he was relieved when Keisha offered hers.

Dennis was so attracted to Keisha he couldn't wait. He called Keisha the very same night he met her. Keisha's in person bravado seemed to resonate over the phone. In fact, Dennis had to initiate each subject or topic when they spoke. Keisha found Dennis physically attractive. Compared to Keisha's usual type of man, Dennis was a square. Keisha was actually attracted to the squareness in Dennis. Keisha worked at the post office, primarily working the front counter.

She was also in school. Keisha had a very busy schedule. But their phone conversations never lasted over 20 minutes per call. Keisha would give only one-word answers to Dennis's job interview style questions. "Yep" "Nope" "Un-huh" was all the feedback Dennis got. Whenever Keisha seemed to be speaking to Dennis about anything of substance, Keisha would actually interrupt herself by constantly screaming commands at her two daughters. Dennis couldn't get a read on her or really a good word in.

After a month they were still no more than telephone tag mates. Dennis was bothered by Keisha's language with her daughters.

She would literally curse them out with the same ferocity in which she cursed out the cashier at the grocery store. What bothered Dennis the most is the vicious verbal attack she'd launch while Dennis was on the phone. Dennis couldn't imagine speaking to his daughter that way.

Keisha had a daughter in the 6th grade and a daughter in the 8th grade. Keisha wouldn't put the phone down or on mute. Instead she'd hold the phone right up to her mouth and scream. Dennis got an earful each time she yelled. Surprisingly enough, Keisha and Dennis went out to dinner every off day they both shared.

There was something about Keisha that kept Dennis guessing. Dennis enjoyed being with Keisha. She attracted a lot of attention with her loudmouth, the way she dressed and her big butt. Everywhere they went men would stare, mouths agape at Keisha's butt which was a phenomenon. When Keisha spoke, her octave would travel to heights where you'd think she was equipped with a volume knob.

At dinner, Keisha only spoke loud and negatively about other women. She was a glass half empty kind of woman. Every time Dennis mentioned anyone or anything not directly concerning Keisha, she'd have a personal pessimistic retort. Keisha had a gorgeous smile resembling the actress Vanessa Bell Calloway with dimples and all. Dennis tried his best to be patient with Keisha. Dennis noticed that Keisha ignorantly loved to perform in public. Much like she did with the cashier when they met.

Dennis began to notice little discrepancies in her character and behavior that he found offensive. Dennis and Keisha seemed to have exciting conversations in person. Keisha made it a point to refer to the waitress as "Hun." Dennis placed his order, but the waitress couldn't put the order in because Keisha kept altering her order in some way. Keisha was attention starved. She seemed to thrive on it. The waitress was finally able to put the order in after countless questions and decision changing substitutions. Keisha had two forms of expression, silence and rage. She was so aggressive, even in agreement her tone and mannerism made Dennis feel as if he was chewing sandpaper.

The more time Dennis spent out with her, the more turned off he grew. Dennis tried to bring up certain things about her that bothered him. His comments gift wrapped in compliments as they were, still met with vicious opposition from Keisha. Whomever had hurt Keisha and made her this way really did a number on her. Dennis began to look forward to their alone time as oppose to going out like they did in the beginning.

Keisha had invited Dennis to her place for dinner. Dennis came by on a Wednesday at 11:00 pm and he was surprised to see Keisha's daughter wide awake on a school night. But it wasn't his place to mention it. Dennis and Keisha began light to heavy petting on the couch. With Keisha's daughters running in and out of the front room, Dennis felt annoyed and uncomfortable.

What struck him as odd was that Keisha wasn't bothered at all by the daughters.

I'm Leaving You For A White Woman

Both daughters were in their night clothes. Both went back and forth to the kitchen and restroom. But mainly to sneak peeks of their mom in action. Dennis selfishly continued smooching with Keisha. He was bothered yes, but not to the point of stopping. As it got later, both agreed that they should call it a night. Dennis and Keisha couldn't be more different.

Unlike with Ruby, Dennis just couldn't keep her attention. Keisha let Dennis know that the type of man she was used to dating was a little rougher around the edges. Some like to refer to such men as thugs. Keshia's record with men was a destructive one. She was quick to roll her neck, ball up her fist and engage in an obscene confrontation verbal or physical, with males or females.

Keisha used her attitude as a defense mechanism. She took out the pain of her past relationships on her present ones. She bragged about never being in love. She saw love as a weakness. The more Dennis tried to become closer emotionally, the harder Keisha would push back. Keisha would look for conflict where there wasn't one. She thrived on it.

Keisha's emotions stayed closed, except when it came to her female friends which she referred to as "Her girls." Keisha was riding with Dennis one Sunday morning doing a little shopping. Dennis was on a personal quest to purchase the perfect vacuum cleaner. They had already gone to two small discount stores. Now it was time to hit the major stores.

Dennis knew this would be an increase in price. Dennis finally decided that he'd get the super deluxe model. He enjoyed being with Keisha on the rare occasions she was quiet. As they were leaving the department store, Keisha recognized one of her daughter's fathers and decided to confront him.

As she began to yell and scream in his face, he just smiled and attempted to walk away. The more he ignored Keisha, the more aggressive she became. Dennis kept trying to take Keisha by the hand but to no avail. She snatched away and continued to walk behind the man as he walked towards the entrance to the store.

Dennis walked away to put the vacuum cleaner in the trunk of his car. Then Dennis ran back to Keisha who was now standing in the doorway. As Dennis approached the doorway, he noticed a strange occurrence. A store security guard had noticed the scene in the parking lot. Now the store security guard was standing between Keisha and Dennis. What was so strange to Dennis was that Keisha wasn't as aggressive. The security guard stood around 5'8" tall. Every time Keisha attempted to speak, the guard merely held up his hand and Keisha would stop on a dime.

Her tone had changed from savagely vicious, to cool calm and collected. Dennis also noticed that the security guard happen to be a white man. The security guard spoke calmly as well as authoritatively while Keisha was on her "Sunday school behavior" as grandma use to say. Her daughter's father walked back into the store while Keisha and Dennis held hands and walked to the car. The whole ordeal lasted about 10 minutes. As Dennis and Keisha drove away, the car was silent. Not even the radio was on. Keisha had a look on her face as if she'd seen a ghost. Keisha's entire demeanor had Dennis even more perplexed than the parking lot scene. He wanted to open up and say something, but he didn't know what to say. So, for nearly the entire ride back to Keisha's place there was silence.

Finally, as they got closer to Keisha's house Dennis opened up in an attempt to not break the ice, but to defrost some of it.

"What was all that about?" Dennis asked. Keisha didn't just respond, she exploded. At first the destination of her torpedoes were directed towards her daughter's father. She lost that obedient child-like demeanor that she had with the white security guard.

Keisha started screaming at the top of her lungs about her youngest daughter's father. She was angry because her last child support check was 1/3 short. She also mentioned that he's married now with a six-month-old son that apparently, he is a better father to.

Dennis felt at that moment Keisha might be still in love with him. He intelligently didn't comment as she was venting in stereo. People in passing cars could hear her even though the windows were up. Then in a flash, Keisha turned her anger towards Dennis. Keisha called Dennis a "punk bitch" for not standing up for her. Her rant re-started as it was in the parking lot before security arrived. As Dennis pulled up at Keisha's house he drove off. Dennis was worried that Keisha was going to take her bad attitude inside with her daughters. So, Dennis decided to lap the block a few times til she cooled off.

Keisha continued to take her frustrations out on Dennis. Keisha told Dennis that he was supposed to fight her daughters' father. Keisha kept calling Dennis everything but his name. She told Dennis that if he were any kind of man that he would have just punched him. Dennis told Keisha that he didn't want to get involved because the guy was her child's father. Also, because they guy didn't seem like he was threatening her.

The insults kept coming. Dennis wanted to address some of the comments Keisha made but he was too scared. The more Dennis ignored Keisha, the louder she became. After a few slow laps around the block they parked in front of her house. As Dennis was trying to calm Keisha down, she picked up her cell phone and called a friend.

Keisha put the telephone on speaker and explained to a friend what had happened. Before she placed the call, Keisha had actually calmed down a little, or so he thought. Keisha's friend re-affirmed Keisha stance on what Dennis should have done.

Now Keisha and her equally loudmouth friend were discussing Dennis's testicles or the lack thereof as if he weren't there. Dennis had reached his breaking point. He told Keisha that it was late, and he had to be at work early tomorrow. The excuse Dennis gave Keisha was only partially true.

He didn't know what to say to calm her down. He figured he'd best just go home. On the way home, Dennis did a lot of soul searching. He and Keisha had clashed on several differences of opinions. Dennis grew angry with himself during his drive home. He was pondering what he may have done to prevent what had occurred.

The whole ordeal had mentally and physically drained Dennis dry. He had nothing left even for himself. Dennis had met Keisha's type before. Women like Keisha have talked many men into the penitentiary and graveyard. Dennis knew involving himself into physical altercation could have ended with jail, death or at the very least lawsuit or loss of job. Dennis' rational mind told him what he did was exactly what he should have done.

Keisha's rant took a lot out of his spirit. He tried to convince himself that Keisha was different. But deep inside he knew she was a typical hood rat. With that post office job and nice house Keisha was a woman who identified more with where she came from, than where she was going.

Keisha was caught up in "Keeping it real." Some of her sayings were "Don't get me started" and "What comes up, comes out." Implying that she had a total lack of self-control. A fact that Dennis couldn't completely swallow because he had just observed Keisha's demeanor with the White security guard at the department store. Keisha was soft spoken, choosing her words carefully and "yes sir" "no sir" when addressing him. It couldn't have been a financial issue because Keisha makes at least twice what that security guard brings home. Dennis could only deduce that Keisha attitude was more selective than reactive.

He witnessed with his own eyes how civilized Keisha could behave. Dennis pondered all night about Keisha. Dennis wasn't the type to call his peers to discuss his personal life or relationship with them. On a rare occasion, he would converse with his sister on the subject of 'today's women.'

Keisha always put her girlfriends above any romantic relationship she was involved in. Even though her friends were compiled of single mother's with multiple baby daddy's and none had ever been married. Still knowing this, Keisha considered and regarded their opinions as law.

Keisha spoke to 'Her girls' with the utmost respect. Sometimes she was playfully familiar with them. Whenever she'd get a call or text from them even during a date, she would always take the call. Keisha thrived off the attention no matter how negative or positive. Keisha drew her strength form her rage, like the Hulk. Before during and after every date, Keisha checked in with her "girls" and gave them blow by blow detail.

Her self-worth was measured by the number of off colored comments and looks she receives. Thus, making her underlined objective "Attention." Keisha was normally in outfits that showed off her enormous butt. Keisha seemed to purposely seek attention from strangers only to respond negatively. This kept her in a constant paradox. A case of her confusing herself.

I'm Leaving You For A White Woman

Keisha seemed to be angry all of the time. When dating Dennis, he noticed that he had to break the ice on all of their dates in order for her to participate in the discussion. No matter how many dates they went on, Keisha seemed to be uneasy and uncomfortable. Conflict and confusion were Keisha's comfort zone.

Dennis felt Keisha was constantly putting an emotional wall between them. Aside from sex and an obvious physical attraction, Dennis felt constant distance. To Keisha being in love meant being weak. Keisha and women like her didn't go on dates, they went to war.

When on a date, from the conversation to sex it was a war of leverage. Keisha wouldn't speak so aggressively when it was just the two of them. One day the two of them were at the park. Dennis had made them a picnic lunch on a blanket. Keisha was so surprised she began kissing and hugging all over Dennis. There wasn't a special occasion. Dennis hadn't stepped up romantically. Keisha had taken pictures of the spread with her cell phone and emailed the pictures to her "Home girls." Dennis didn't seem to mind this particular gesture. This was the first time she'd text something positive about him.

Dennis was willing to try with Keisha. Just in an instance, Dennis made a startling discovery. He was wearing tennis shoes, she was wearing tennis shoes. He was wearing blue jeans. She was waring blue jeans. He was wearing a t-shirt. She was wearing a t-shirt. It hit Dennis like a ton of bricks. He felt he was dating a homeboy.

41

There was no difference except she has a vagina. He realized that's why even with no apparent emotional connection Dennis had sex with Keisha only so often. During sex is the only time Dennis saw Keisha in a feminine light. Keisha's natural demeanor was so aggressive it came off as masculine. That was the way Keisha showed she cared.

Dennis didn't see it that way. Because she was so zero to sixty with her temper, he was on constant eggshells, whenever he dealt with Keisha. Even though she never regarded Dennis's feelings in the same regard. Dennis couldn't get past the department store incident or the "punk bitch" comment. As much as he tried to get past it, he just couldn't. After that day, he put her permanently in the too much drama category.

At the park they enjoyed a game of basketball with each other. Keisha had a pretty face, a gorgeous body and a smile that could melt the North Pole. But no mater how long they dated, Keisha never really took Dennis into her heart. No one could penetrate that fortress of solitude.

Dennis knew he wasn't the only guy dating Keisha. Even though that's what he convinced himself of. Dennis wanted something more, something new. But he still wasn't ready to give up Keisha 100%. One day Dennis and Keisha had met for lunch. It was during his lunch break. The two of them were enjoying some Chinese food. Keisha had gotten a text that put an instant smile on her face. She kept commenting verbally on the text as if she wanted him to comment.

Dennis was determined not to comment. Judging from Keisha's reaction she was texting a man. Keisha was again putting on a show. Dennis was getting more and more upset with each passing minute. This time Dennis felt he needed to speak on it. He also knew that a confrontation is exactly what Keisha wanted. Dennis opened his mouth to make a comment and Keisha immediately put her left hand up in his face.

Keisha was always flying off the handle about someone disrespecting her, yet she seldom showed respect towards anyone. Dennis felt her entire ghetto persona was all by choice since that day at the department store with the white security guard. He'd also been present when Keisha's job would call her in.

Sometimes Keisha got called into work on weekends. It was time and a half overtime. Her speech during these calls rivaled a press secretary. Her job had her undivided attention. But this time he could tell it was a personal call. She finally hung up the phone and began to gather her things.

Dennis ask Keisha who was the call from? Keisha frowned with her forehead wrinkled and smiled at the same time. "Why?" Was her response. Dennis got up to leave. At that precise moment, Keisha went from zero to sixty and began shouting obscenities at Dennis. Dennis knew his question would invoke a response. But not in a million years did he expect her to take such an aggressive tone with him. Dennis had seen her go off on others and he wanted no parts of that. He shook his head and attempted to walk away.

Keisha blocked the door and increased her ferociousness. She stood there with both hands on her hips and her neck going from side to side and in circular motion. Her voice went from clear and high pitched, to loud and raspy. It wasn't until a couple approached the door to get in, did she move. That's when Dennis left. Her rant continued to the parking lot and to Dennis's car.

Keisha and Dennis were both on break for lunch, so they met up at the restaurant separately. As Dennis drove off, Keisha went and got in her car. Dennis was afraid that Keisha would follow him back to his job. But she didn't. She drove back to work.

Keisha's job was very important to her. She had just gotten a raise and a lot of envious co-workers wanted her spot. Dennis had decided not to call or see her again. He figured he'd rather be alone than deal with the huge chip on Keisha's shoulder. This wasn't like Dennis to put up with such behavior.

Catherine was the woman he admitted made a fool of him. That was only because of his daughter Princess. Dennis did all he could to forget about Keisha. Keisha was the best sexual experience of his life. The only time Keisha was submissive with Dennis was during sex.

Dennis and Keisha had sex often for that reason. Keisha felt Dennis was whipped because she felt she had diamonds where her thighs meet. Keisha measured her power from the number of socially interested parties of the opposite sex. This puts her in perpetual whoredom.

I'm Leaving You For A White Woman

Or a constant air of single and on the market currently. Even though she knew Dennis is dating her exclusively. Keisha wasn't looking for love in its traditional sense. Her main objective was companionship. Dennis wasn't in love either. But he wanted to be. Out of all his past relationships he wanted Keisha the most.

Keisha put Dennis in a constant position where he found himself apologizing for his own masculinity. Dennis had bent over backwards to please Keisha. Bending over backwards is uncomfortable, literally. Days had gone by since Dennis and Keisha spoke.

Dennis pondered the how's and why's the entire weekend. He attempted to call Keisha, but he got nothing but her voice mail. Dennis was conflicted. He was falling for a woman he couldn't stand. The conflict lied within himself. Dennis's lust for Keisha drove him to call, but his pride and self-respect made him hang up prematurely.

Dennis had disdain for Keisha's typical behavior. He felt her response at the Chinese restaurant went above and beyond the norm.

Keisha unknowingly had a deep-rooted hatred of men. Keisha would break up with men before they dumped her. A subconscious cycle of self-sabotage. These men would not be in the process of leaving Keisha. Keisha's defense mechanism was distance.

In her mind, love was a vulnerability, a weakness. Keisha had no problems being vulnerable, open and honest with her female friends. Dennis wasn't ready to call it quits.

He wasn't angry at Keisha. Slightly upset, but not angry and not upset enough to call it over. He figured he'd give Keisha some time to cool off. Dennis called his sister to maybe obtain some insight. He explained the entire scenario to his sister Dana Alexander.

Dennis and Dana were five years apart and were thick as thieves. Dennis considered Dana his best friend. They used each other to confide in whenever one or the other were down. Dana wasn't a teacher like her brother. Dana was a city bus driver. She, like her brother, worked the morning shift. So, on most evenings they'd call one another.

Usually Dana would call Dennis after 7 pm to initiate the conversation. Dana would bring Dennis her man troubles and Dennis would do his best to provide the male perspective. But in recent years their relationship grew distant. Dana was now married with a 3yr old son. She was in a strong and health relationship with her husband.

In recent months it was Dennis with the questions for Dana. He figured she must have answers of enlightenment since her marriage seemed productive and peaceful. After Dennis explained the Chinese restaurant incident in detail, Dana could offer little to no advice. What little she did offer seemed to lean more towards Keisha's side.

Dana didn't fully believe Dennis. She felt that Dennis had exaggerated when describing Keisha's reaction. Dana wrote Keisha's behavior off on hormones. Dennis allowed himself to believe Dana 100% and went with her reasoning.

I'm Leaving You For A White Woman

He wanted Dana to re-enforce what he was already thinking and feeling. Dennis didn't so much miss Keisha as he wanted an explanation over what he did so wrong. Dennis grew up with both parents. When he hit junior high school, his parents were divorced. Dennis and Dana stayed with Florence. Money was tight, and Dennis saw his mother and sister work hard to keep the family house.

When both parents were together, and in the home, there was a surplus of income and luxuries. After the divorce, Dennis's father moved out and moved on. He took his ample salary with him. His salary alone counted for 2/3 of the household income. With Mr. Alexander gone, Florence had to take the wheel and become the man of the house. The primary breadwinner.

This left Dana in the role of woman of the house or secondary parent. Mr. and Mrs. Alexander had socked away quite the nest egg for Dana's college education. That college fund was rapidly depleted after Mr. Alexander's departure. Dana was forced due to circumstances to enter the workforce as soon as she graduated high school. Florence and Dana worked hard and by the time Dennis graduated high school, his college fund was ample.

Dennis's father, mother, aunt and sister were at his college graduation. They were all so proud of him. Dennis was grateful for his family's sacrifice, but it came with the heavy heart of guilt. Dennis, even in gratitude, never felt he gave enough to his sister or mother. Dennis harbored resentment towards his father. In his eyes he abandoned the family and left them in turmoil.

Dennis knew not the ramifications surrounding his parent's separation and later divorce. Dennis was left with the aftermath of their decision. He saw his mother over worked and underpaid. He saw his sister defer her own dream of higher education for sake of the family.

Dennis graduated college with honors. He excelled on the basketball court and the classroom. Because of the sacrifices of his family, Dennis took his education and activities seriously. Whenever his mother or sister needed anything, Dennis would drop what he was doing and consider their needs first.

His mother Florence used this guilt as a weapon to control Dennis. Constant feelings of guilt behind her struggle affected him even in his current relationships. Dennis deep down inside felt that if he went against women, that he was in fact going against his mom and sister. Dennis, unaware of this fact didn't realize that this pattern was self-destructive or relationship suicide. He was dooming himself before he could start without knowing.

Catherine, the mother of his daughter would play on this. She knew which buttons to push and how far. Dennis's free will was plagued with turmoil. The fact that Dennis's mom Florence was usually on Catherine's side for self-satisfying reasons created confusion and conflict within him.

Without ever saying it, Dennis felt personally responsible for his sister Dana not going to college. He was primarily an athlete first and a student second. Dana was an A student. She had also built up quite an elective resume'.

I'm Leaving You For A White Woman

With her glee club, band, volleyball, and student body treasurer position. She was looking at top colleges around the country. Dana made up her mind in her senior year that she was going to get a job and help her mother. Dennis was determined not to let his family down. Dennis blamed his father for his mother's pain and his sister's deferred dream. This misplaced guilt allowed Dennis to be taken advantage of in many of his relationships. This put Dennis in a state of anxiety and shame whether he was in the right or wrong. Dennis felt the more he gave to himself, the more he took from his mom and sister. This was Dennis's truth.

After a lengthy session with his councilor, Dennis was indeed drained yet again. Bringing up old memories of Keisha stirred up once dead emotions. Dennis though he was over Keisha but after the session with his therapist he realized he missed her.

The thought of Dennis getting back with Catharine never crossed his mind. He found himself in a position of competing with Catherine for his mother's loyalty and love.

After 3 weeks, Dennis decided to call Keisha. As soon as he heard her voice, he immediately felt regret. Dennis was as nice as he could be. Keisha gave polite, one-word answers. He could tell she was still mad. Keisha began laughing with someone else who was in the background edging her on.

Dennis drove to see his mother. He often checked on her during the week. He pulls up only to find Catharine's car parked out front. Dennis stomach instantly filled with butterflies. He parked behind Catherine's car. He just sat there parked. Dennis was doing all he could to calm his nerves in an attempt to go inside. Thinking maybe Princess was with Catherine, Dennis worked up the nerve to enter after 10 minutes of prayer and meditation.

Dennis walked in and saw his mother playing with Princess. Catherine was in the restroom. Dennis began to pick up Princess. Princess was so excited to see Dennis she began laughing uncontrollably. Catherine emerged from the bathroom shocked to see Dennis.

She was polite whenever she was around Dennis's mom Florence. Catherine spoke nothing of the approaching court date. When Dennis brought it up, Florence would get scared that Catherine would take the baby and leave. Out of fear, Florence lashed out against Dennis. As Florence was yelling at Dennis, Catherine gathered Princess's toys and they left. Leaving Dennis at his mom's home in mid-argument.

Usually Dennis was as delicate and graceful as a ballerina when it came to his mom or sister. But Dennis was never able to keep his cool when it came to his child. Florence continued to minimize, deny and blame Dennis for the entire situation. Florence lashed out of her own personal pain.

Her pain stemmed from the rejection and betrayal she felt from Dennis father. From a position of spinsterhood watching in silence as Dennis's father personal life continue to flourish

I'm Leaving You For A White Woman

while hers stayed dormant later festering into a
bitter private hell.

After over a decade of living alone, Princess
represented a new beginning for her. Whenever
Florence defended Catherine's malicious actions,
she felt she was defending herself. She saw Princess
as her new beginning. In Dennis's mind, he thought
his mom was crazy. He often spoke about it with his
sister in confidence. He was in fear that his mother
was suffering from early signs of dementia.

Dennis love for his mother was becoming
more and more expensive. It was wearing him down
to the point that the mere mention of her name
instantly depressed him. The only person that
seemed to slightly understand his position was his
sister.

Since she's gotten married, their
conversations became far and few between.
Whenever she could she'd lend an ear to the perils
of Dennis's personal life. Dennis's self-esteem
seemed to be under constant attack. His therapist
could do only so much. His therapist was doing all
she could to unlock Dennis's inner self. She wanted
Dennis to find the strength within himself to solve
his own problems and issues that seem to be
determining factors in his life.

Florence and Dennis continued to argue to
the point where both were now screaming at one
another. Florence's stance on Catherine's side had
begun to take its toll on Dennis. He left his mom's
house and drove straight to the gym. He kept his
gym bag and a change of clothes in his trunk.

Dennis didn't go to work out. He just went to get in the steam room, sauna and jacuzzi. After the gym he drove home. When Dennis got home, the first thing he did was call his mother Florence to apologize. Florence informed Dennis that Catherine had been bringing Princess by every day since she had Dennis served with Court papers.

Dennis's stomach dropped when he heard that. This was because since the papers were served, Dennis hadn't spent time with his daughter. Before he was served, Dennis had Princess every weekend. He had no idea why he was being summonsed to court. Catherine and Dennis had been on friendly terms up until he was served.

Every day without his daughter seemed like weeks. Each passing week seemed like months. Dennis's every thought was on his daughter. He couldn't help but feel that he was being betrayed somehow by his mom. Florence told Dennis that she was talking to Catherine every day trying to soften her up.

Dennis didn't believe his mother, but he wanted to so badly. So, he made himself swallow this pill. Dennis didn't want to talk about these present issues at his next counseling session.

Dennis's sister Dana called to check on him. She was worried about how he was holding up. Dana had also put in for a day off so she could go to court with him. She didn't want Dennis to feel that he had no allies. When Dana told Dennis about her going to court with him his entire mood changed. He knew Dana would get a chance to see Catherine with her own eyes.

I'm Leaving You For A White Woman

Dana would babysit Princess often while Dennis and Catherine were together. Dennis was up late nights working on mid-terms and grading papers. He was preparing mid-terms for his students while he was studying for his own. He was working on his master's degree. Going to night school 3 days a week, his calendar was full.

He did all he could to keep his mind focused on his work. Dennis reported the details of his counselling sessions to his sister and sometimes his mother. He knew that those details would make its way to Catherine.

Up until now, Dennis and Catherine had toyed with the idea of getting back together. When Dennis suggested couple's counseling Catherine did a complete 180° turn. She seemed somehow to be attacking Dennis. These attacks Dennis viewed especially malicious because it was totally unprovoked.

I'm Leaving You For A White Woman

Chapter 4

La Ronda was a pretty woman. She was bi-racial and seemed carefree. La Ronda was sort of an enigma to Dennis. Her father was Mexican, and her mother was African American. Her parents had been together since they were in their early 20's. La Ronda had an okay body, a pretty face and the straightest whitest teeth Dennis had ever seen.

La Ronda had gone to high school with Dennis. They never dated or really spoke in high school. In fact, Dennis never had the guts to approach La Ronda. He remembered she was always smiling and or laughing with her crew of 3 other girls of similar backgrounds. Others referred them as 'The Privileged Girls.' Some called them stuck up. La Ronda wasn't particularly rich. Her parents were still married both with careers.

Her mother was a social worker and her father owned a construction company. She was an only child who still lived at home in the bedroom she grew up in. She had never married nor had any children. Dennis saw La Ronda out of all places at the supermarket.

He noticed her instantly and said "Hello." La Ronda smiled, lightly waved and said "Hello" back. Dennis left her in the produce section and continued shopping. He was working up the nerve to say something, anything. He thought to himself, 'It's been over 10 years.' He grabbed a few more items, worked up the heart to approach her, then headed back towards the produce section. La Ronda wasn't there. Dennis was angry at himself for not speaking when he saw her. He felt he'd never get this chance again. On the other hand, he exhaled a sigh of relief. He imagined himself embarrassingly striking out.

As he turned the corner, he looked down each isle and still, no La Ronda. So, Dennis got in the shortest line. La Ronda came right behind him with her basket. She asked Dennis "Where do I know you from?" Dennis face lit up. Those six words were more than she'd ever said to him in school. La Ronda was the head cheerleader in high school. Rumor has it, her boyfriend was a super star football player from a rival high school at the time.

Dennis reminded La Ronda that they went to high school together. She actually remembered his face, but not his name. Dennis walked her to the car. Before he could ask for her number, she offered hers.

She wrote it on a scrap of paper and told Dennis to call her sometime. Dennis smiled and he had already mapped out their first date in his mind. He did his best not to look nervous. Dennis wasn't even aware at how wide he was smiling.

La Ronda had a way of making people smile. He approached everyday situations gently. She had the air of royalty. She was as fine as she thought she was. Since the age of 5, La Ronda has been told how beautiful she was. She was a model by age 12. She did a few commercials in high school but none since.

Dennis saw La Ronda giving him her number as a feather in is cap. He couldn't tell if he was actually attracted to her, or what she represented back in high school. Either or, Dennis was thrilled about the idea. As he remembered, La Ronda never spoke to him or any guys at the school. Only fellow cheerleaders.

When Dennis got home, he called his best friend Eddie. Eddie went to high school with Dennis and La Ronda. Eddie would remember La Ronda mainly because Eddie played on the basketball team. Eddie and Dennis discussed La Ronda all night. They were as giddy and as chatty as two junior high school girls.

Dennis wanted to talk to La Ronda but wouldn't call her the first night he got her number. At the same time, he knew a woman like La Ronda must get propositioned a lot. He didn't want to wait too long, and he didn't want to seem desperate. After the break-up with Keisha, Dennis confidence had taken a great blow.

Dennis wanted so bad to tell his therapist about La Ronda. Even though his therapist had no interest in him sexually, personally or socially. Somehow it mattered to Dennis. Dennis was being treated in his therapy sessions. These sessions took a lot out of Dennis. Dennis was open and honest as he could be with his therapist, but Dennis felt weak and vulnerable during his sessions. Dennis didn't want her to think he was a chump.

Before Dennis called La Ronda, he wanted to see his therapist first. Dennis wanted some advice on what to say and what to do. Dennis went to his next therapy session with validation on his mind. He wanted to report to his therapist that his self-confidence was back. In his mind, La Ronda's phone number somehow represented victory. Dennis called La Ronda two days after he got her number.

He had Eddie waiting on a phone call. Eddie was interested in how Dennis first date with the legendary La Ronda would be. Dennis had called her earlier to set up their first date. Dennis finally called La Ronda after he got off work and left the gym. It was 6pm give or take and La Ronda let it ring three times before she answered. She sounded so excited to hear Dennis's voice. La Ronda had just gotten out of the shower. She had explained that she was wet and nude because she had just gotten out of the shower to catch the phone.

La Ronda was extremely receptive. She told him that she hadn't gone out in a while and was curious to where they were going. Dennis was still wrapping his head around the fact she was on the phone with him while wet and nude. La Ronda told Dennis that she would go out with him but stated that next time she prefers a few days advance notice. He completely understood and didn't find her particular request out of the ordinary.

Dennis pulled up on time. Because it was such short notice, he didn't have a date planned. He was looking and smelling good. When Dennis got to the door, he was holding a dozen red roses. La Ronda's father answered the door. He was a short Latino man. He stood about 5'4". Then La Ronda's mother came to the door. She was a light-skinned black woman around 5'10". Both seemed overjoyed to see Dennis as if they'd been expecting him.

Their attitudes took a lot of the edge off. Dennis returned their smiles with his own. Dennis was seated by La Ronda's father in the living room. Her mother returned upstairs while her father questioned him. Dennis took one look around and he was intrigued. The living room, couch and love seat were covered in plastic. There was a bowl full of candy on the living room table which appeared to be all stuck together. The home smelled of cinnamon and potpourri. In the corner was an old styled sewing machine.

The house was huge. It was at least 6 bedrooms or more. The home had wall to wall white shag carpeting and 1970's style velvet wallpaper. In another corner was a wicker chair swing. La Ronda came downstairs in a yellow sundress. Dennis stood up and presented her with flowers. La Ronda's face lit up as she took the roses. Both parents walked them out.

In high school, students would ask her all of the time what race was she? She would always answer black. Dennis asked about her Mexican father. La Ronda said her father was Cuban, not Mexican. His family was mainly still in Cuba except for his sister in Miami. La Ronda use to spend summers with her when she was younger. La Ronda was mostly raised around her mother's side of the family. They were from Cleveland Ohio. La Ronda was raised all of her life in the same house. Dennis found this peculiar.

Dennis took La Ronda to a popular bar and grill with video games, pool tables, darts, and air hockey. La Ronda felt right at home. She immediately ran to a virtual motorcycle machine built for two. They were both enjoying themselves as if they were back in high school. At the table they both shared a plate of hot wings.

Dennis ordered a beer and La Ronda ordered a diet 7up with a cherry and lime in it. La Ronda began to give Dennis a hard time about ordering a beer. She said she wouldn't ride in the car with him if he drank one drop of alcohol. Dennis laughed it off then to find out she was serious.

Turns out La Ronda's upbringing was deeply religious. The house and atmosphere started to make sense to Dennis. La Ronda wasn't stuck up or arrogant in high school, just extremely sheltered. La Ronda still lived at home. She wasn't married and had no children. Her parents treated her like a child. When the order came, La Ronda challenged Dennis to a race to see who could finish the hot wings the fastest.

I'm Leaving You For A White Woman

La Ronda's life was controlled by her parents. Her bedroom was still as it was when she was in high school. Right down to The Backstreet Boys poster on her wall. Dennis drank his beer right in front of La Ronda. La Ronda gave him the silent treatment. Dennis wanted to take La Ronda to the movies after the bar. That was when La Ronda said she had to be home by 10pm.

Dennis couldn't believe how La Ronda lived. She was over 30 years old, but she seemed as though she had been frozen in time. Dennis took her home. He walked her to the door. La Ronda rang the doorbell. She had no key. Both of her parents answered the door. A few seconds after they opened the door. La Ronda kissed Dennis on the cheek, smiled and went into the house.

La Ronda's father shook Dennis's hand and thanked him for returning his daughter home at a respectable hour. Dennis went to work Monday with La Ronda on his mind. It was mid-term week for his 11th graders. Dennis had to administer the test. The school's vice principal Mr. Bill Toliver had popped in to see how the first-year teacher Dennis Alexander was doing.

Mr. Toliver was impressed. Dennis was doing well at his teaching job. Unfortunately, he was neglecting his studies for his master's degree. He had so much on his plate. Dennis went straight to his therapist at the end of the day. La Ronda was still on his mind when he walked in

Dennis was explaining his date to his therapist, but she was not interested. She wanted to dig deeper into his past. She was doing all she could

to get him to get use to the idea of group sessions.
Dennis didn't mind the idea, but he made it known
to her that he preferred one on one counseling.

Dennis had to turn his cell phone off. La
Ronda had called him 3 times in a 30-minute
period. He texted her 'I'm with my doctor.' La
Ronda was unlike any woman Dennis ever dated.
He was turned off by her household. It was a bit too
old fashioned for him to deal with. But La Ronda
was interested in Dennis.

La Ronda lived a sheltered life. She seemed
wholesome and innocent. A totally different type of
speed for Dennis. Dennis decided to just be friends
for now with La Ronda. At least until they date a
little more. He still wasn't sure if he was over
Keisha yet. He didn't want to end up treating La
Ronda as a rebound chick.

Dennis sat on the therapist couch. His
therapy/counseling sessions were 1/3 counseling 1/3
therapy and 1/3 hypnosis. Dennis was enjoying his
freedom from Ruby. Because of her age, it put him
in a boytoy category. He was defiantly the Beta in
the relationship, leaving Ruby to be the Alpha
between the two of them. Dennis had once told his
therapist that living with Ruby was equivalent to
always wearing a tight turtleneck sweater.

Dr Sylvia was slowly, but surely getting to
the root of the problem. Her goal was for Dennis to
recognize the root, uproot it, then replant a healthier
tree so his happiness could grow. She saw love and
tenderness deep inside of him like a rose. But a rose
unable to grow because it's being chocked by the
weeds around and within it.

Other than his sister, Dennis would confide as honestly as he could with his best friend Tasha. Tasha was a certain kind of special. Dennis couldn't love her as a mate if he tried. Tasha was a brown-skinned woman around 5'7". She was thick but still had a decent shape. Tasha was insecure and self-conscious about her weight. She was the darker completed of her three sisters.

When describing anyone she always started with the skin tone even before the sex. She would say things like "That dark skin girl was at the counter." Tasha used outdated terms like "Good hair." Dennis noticed that Tash would comment negatively about every light-skinned or racially mixed woman she saw while they were together.

Because of her complexion, she felt she was just okay looking no matter how many times Dennis called her beautiful. Tasha represented the typical black woman that Dennis was growing to despise. But Tasha was the type of woman he was used to. She was like his loud auntie Daphne.

His mother's sister Daphne was Dennis's favorite aunt. To a degree, Dennis feared Tasha. He wasn't afraid of her in the literal sense. He was more so afraid of what she'd say or do. Her favorite phrase was "Don't get me started." Implying that she had no control over her actions once her emotions came into play. Like some sort of animal, a beast, a runaway freight train with no conductor and no breaks.

This is what's referred to as a "strong black woman" in the black community. A term that made Dennis's skin crawl.

Any activity typical or stereotypical upset Dennis in an acute way. It touched a nerve deep inside of him. Dennis was a young black man who grew up with both of his parents in the home for the most part. Despite hard times, he still graduated from college and now he was working on his master's degree. Most of his life he's been dumped into categories he didn't deserve. The question he posed to himself was 'Why do I keep choosing these types of women?'

Certain attitudes seemed pertinent in urban American cities. Dennis had grown to accept the verbal and psychological abuse from black women. Dennis's plight represented a microcosm of a much bigger problem. An epidemic if you will. The mere memories of Tasha stirred up a lot of memories. Things he wanted to forget. Sometimes knowing where you've been can help to point you to where you need to go. People fear what they don't understand.

Dennis considered all women to be simply complexed. In therapy, Dennis was learning how not to blame himself. The therapist was trying to get Dennis to forgive himself and release his misplaced guilt. The whole point of therapy was so Dennis and Catherine could repair their torn relationship. The therapist saw a bigger problem and saw Catherine as a minor piece of a much bigger puzzle. He was using the sessions as a way of healing.

Tasha and Dennis didn't date much so to speak. They did however spend almost every night together. Tasha was bitter and pessimistic. She and Dennis would play videogames, watch sports and gossip about reality tv shows together. They were as close as siblings.

Tasha reminded Dennis of most of the women in his family. Dennis' mother never liked Tasha. Even though she claimed to. Dennis first met Tasha through his aunt Daphne. Daphne worked with Tasha at the cable company. Daphne was Tasha's direct supervisor. Daphne and Tasha started going to lunch together. They had known each other for years before Daphne had approached Tasha with the idea of dating her nephew. The problem was Dennis was trying to make it work with Catherine at the time.

Tasha was patient. At first, she and Dennis started out as just friends. They both shared a love of No Limit Hold-em Poker. They would play cards all night. Tasha had talked Dennis into entering a tournament. Tasha had made it to the 5th round and received a trophy. Dennis too, as far as the 2nd round. He received a small plaque for participation.

The two of them had developed a bond that would last the ages. Tasha was the woman that Dennis would call to discuss his issues with Catherine. Over time, the inevitable happened. It was on a Friday night, during one of Catherine's and Dennis breaks. Everyone around them knew that it would eventually happen except for the two of them.

Dennis had come over one night to discuss his problems with Tasha. They sat at the table and played cards. Rumor has it there was alcohol involved. Tasha had gone thru a few one-night stands at the time. She had no one in her life seriously since her son's father. Up until that night, Tasha and Dennis never as much hugged.

It started with a kiss in the kitchen and led to the couch, hallway, shower and bedroom. They made love the entire night until the morning with and unsaid mutual pact. Neither one them would ever do this again with the other one. They both valued their years of friendship with respect. It was two people hurting who decided to heal each other.

Tasha held an unfair advantage when it came to Dennis. Tasha was his shoulder to cry on, so she knew all of his innermost secrets. She knew what made him tick. What made him laugh or cry. So, when it came to Dennis's feelings, no one knew him better. Tasha knew the Alexander family well.

Dennis's mom Florence would try and encourage Dennis to be with Tasha. Florence use to drop hints and say things like she wished he would find a good girl like Tasha. She would say it in front of Tasha and Dennis putting them both on the spot. This would make them both uncomfortable. Especially after they had sex with each other. Both of them agreed to keep it just between the two of them. At least for the sake of their friendship.

Dennis loved Tasha as a friend but there were things about Tasha that he didn't agree with. Their personalities clashed often. They differed on politics, religion, child rearing, etc. Tasha was like a sister to Dennis. Dennis was like an uncle to Tasha's son. But when they all went out together people would stare.

You could see their minds wondering in an attempt to make sense of it all. Tasha's son was half white and half black. Dennis was more of a father to him than his birth father.

The white man that got Tasha pregnant was married. His name was Mark Wells. He and Tasha met on the internet. Mark told Tasha upfront that he was married. He described it as a loveless marriage. Mark gained the sympathetic ear of Tasha and she first felt sorry for him, then befriended him. They communicated via the internet only at first. Mark would be on social media while at work. He and Tasha went from strictly messaging to texting to sexting.

Tasha was raised in such a way Dennis would have never thought she'd date a married man. Mark seemed to light up Tasha's life. Mark would call her from a second cell phone he kept in the glove compartment in his car. Tasha was told not to call Mark and she didn't. Mark would call her, but she wasn't to ever call him.

Tasha would wait patiently until Mark had a chance to sneak away and call her to set up rendezvous. Mark got the chance to pretend he was a secret agent. It was fun to him. Tasha use to brag about Mark as if he were the second coming of Jesus. Tasha had a boyfriend before she met Mark. But as soon as Mark and Tasha met face to face Tasha just dumped her boyfriend with no question and no warning.

Dennis and Tasha didn't agree with one another when it came to Mark. Dennis felt Mark was rude, disrespectful and condescendingly arrogant. Dennis had a great deal of respect for Tasha, and Mark's disrespect rubbed Dennis the wrong way. Tasha's pet peeve was guys who would pop up without calling.

But when it came to Mark, all of her rules, her do's and don'ts were modified. Tasha use to push everything to the side and back burner when it came to Mark. Mark's interest in Tasha was purely sexual. Mark would point out to Tasha that she was his first and only black girl. Tasha use to repeat this to Dennis. She actually would brag about the fact. In some way it made her feel special.

Out of the blue one-day Mark just stopped calling and coming over. She did get text messages every now and then. Tasha never put child support on Mark. Neither did she call or show up at his home or job. Dennis and Tasha spoke candidly about everything.

Tasha was one of the few people who knew he was seeing a therapist. But Tasha regarded herself ½ Dennis's play sister and ½ his counselor. Tasha and Dennis rarely went out with both of their children. Tasha would claim that it didn't look right. Dennis had begun to notice that Tasha only dated light-skinned men. She dated Latino and white as often as she could. If she ever dated a black man, he had to be mixed or very light-skinned.

Dennis as a dark brown black man felt personally rejected. Tasha made sure that Dennis wore a condom on their one-night rendezvous. But she made sure Mark didn't wear one. Tasha didn't just want a baby. She wanted a light-skinned baby specifically. She and Dennis would debate over their views and agreed to disagree.

Chapter 5

Dennis couldn't help but notice her obvious double standard when it came to Tasha's treatment of white or light skinned men and men of Dennis and her own complexion. These were views shared by Tasha's family but not exclusively. Dennis being a dark-skinned black man, he wasn't a stranger to that kind of same race discrimination from black girls of his own shared complexion.

Dennis did a good job not judging Tasha by her opinions on the subject. After all, everyone is entitled to one. But sometimes Dennis couldn't help it. In the back of his mind at times he found it hard to remain quiet, neutral. Dennis loved Tasha like a sister. People who knew them assumed that because Dennis dated a lot, and wasn't with Catherine, that he was afraid of commitment.

One-night, Dennis and Tasha were discussing talk shows and relationships in general. Tasha told Dennis that she purposely had unprotected sex with Mark, so she would possibly have a biracial baby.

Dennis had figured as much because he had spent so much time with Tasha. They even use to go to the gym together at one time.

Dennis felt somewhat sorry for Tasha. She was a beautiful woman who had been thoroughly convinced by her family that she was ugly. Only because she was dark skinned. Tasha never actually said she wanted a "racially mixed" baby. She said she wanted a 'pretty baby.' Dennis knew that to her that meant the same thing. Dennis recalled a conversation they were having when Tasha said her, and Dennis would make an ugly baby because they were both "Too black" as she put it.

Dennis was not a stranger to black women with this type of attitude towards hair and complexion. He had grown up hearing terms like "good hair" meaning straight hair and "pretty eyes' meaning light-eyes. He's even heard it in his own home. Dennis discovered growing up how important hair is to black women. He had actually seen his sister Dana "sleeping pretty." Sleeping pretty is when a black girl actually sleeps sitting up or on all fours in an attempt to keep from altering her hair style from a weave.

As a kid, Dennis recalled laughing to himself when he first noticed his sister doing it. He compared it to an Iguana sitting perfectly still to fool potential prey. Her head propped up and posed. Whenever Tasha tells Dennis she's getting her har "fixed" he knew that means permed or straightened. Whenever she says she's getting her hair "done" he knew that means a weave. Tasha never wore her natural hair in public.

Unless it was completely covered with a scarf. Tasha would tell Dennis she needed a real man. Dennis would often feel the pain of her plight and fix her up with friends of his. Tasha would turn into a living stereo type in an attempt to push them away. She would purposely try to anger them. She'd take a contrary stance on every topic brought up in order to spark debate and conflict.

Tasha wore fake nails, fake hair, fake jewelry and on occasion color contact lenses. But she claimed verbally that she was "too real" for most men. Dennis never confronted Tasha about her views. But her views did strike a nerve sometimes. To Dennis, Tasha hated being black. Therefore, hated black men.

On the rare occasion when she dated a black man, she acted if she was doing "the poor negro race" a favor. Tasha wore ridiculous 30-inch weaves. When speaking, she often would flip, twirl and even play with her false hair. This is something Dennis noticed about black women and their obvious hatred for their natural hair. A lot of the weave wearers flip their fake hair around, constantly playing in it with their fingers.

He personally felt it was pathetic on their part. Dennis and his sister Dana use to have friendly debates about it. Dana's point was today's society demands straight hair for acceptance. She felt that black men wouldn't want a black woman with their natural hair. Dennis would accuse her of a self-hating cop out. Dennis points were: If society says you're ugly with your natural hair, why do you listen? Society says: don't drink and drive, don't smoke, drive over 65mps, exercise daily, eat lean meats and vegetables etc. He figured that out of all things to obey from society, why obey the one thing that says, 'You're inferior?'

Dennis rejected Dana's argument on the subject. Dennis stated that black men have been attracted to black women long before the inventions of the hot comb, weave or extensions. Dennis would claim black women do it because they themselves find it more attractive. Dennis felt black women don't obey the black man on any subject period. So why would they all of a sudden obey them on the subject of 'their hair?'

Tasha would use the word "black" as the ultimate insult. In arguments she would say things like "shut yo black ass up." And things like "you fat, black, so and so." Tasha wouldn't go out in the summer without a hat in fear that the sun would make her darker. She equated being darker with getting uglier.

Every time she saw a light-skinned or white male between the ages of 20-35 she'd comment on how cute or fine he was. As long as he wasn't old or fat. She would pronounce it "Foine." And she would pronounce the word 'foine' in a kind of moaning slow southern drawl when she said it.

There were dark skinned black men that Tasha was sexually attracted to. But she would say things like "He's handsome but we can't have children." Dennis, knowing Tasha, would ask why? She'd say because he's too black. She'd say things like "I'm black enough" referring to her own skin tone. Even though Dennis and Tasha were only friends it didn't matter. Those comments would hurt Dennis's feelings. Tasha was making Dennis feel the same hurt that she claimed she felt growing up darker than her family members. But Dennis noticed that her love for the beauty for light-skinned men didn't spill over onto light skinned women.

Tasha hated light skinned girls. She hated to see black men with white women. Even though she wanted a white man herself, and she deliberately had a baby with a white man. The paradox, contradiction and hypocrisy would stagger the strongest mind.

At the mall in the food court one Saturday morning Dennis and Tasha were hanging out. While they were eating, Tasha and Dennis would eye-buy and people watch. They'd comment on funny or quirky things they'd notice. Dennis had more of a brother/sister relationship with Tasha than his own sister Dana.

Dennis noticed her comments on light-skinned black women. "She thinks she's cute" was one of her comments often used. She would just stare with her lip turned up as if she smelt something that stinks. The comments would be malicious as if the light-skinned woman had done something to her personally.

Tasha, and women like her suffered greatly in silence of poor self-image. Dennis to a certain degree felt sorry for her. He thought how awful it must be to live in constant pain perpetually self-produced. What others thought of her was very important to Tasha. Because of the texture of Tasha's son's hair, she didn't cut it.

She kept his 'good hair' (as she put it) long, in braids or ponytail. But when people confused him for a girl, she'd get angry. Dennis knew Tasha, so he never commented on her son's hair. He knew that would end in conflict. Tasha's son had Mark's last name. Even though he never signed the birth certificate nor acknowledged his existence. With that being said, Tasha still let him come by about once every other month for sex. Tasha never took any aggressive action against Mark.

Tasha had a friend named Jasmine. After being Dennis' shoulder to cry on for years. Tasha felt she knew him best. Tasha felt he'd connect well with her friend Jasmine. Tasha felt that Catherine didn't appreciated Dennis and didn't deserve him. Just as Dennis wanted to see Tasha happy. Tasha wanted the same for Dennis.

Tasha and Jasmine met in hair school. Tasha dropped out early, but Jasmine finished. Jasmine eventually opened her own shop. Jasmine was openly bisexual. She hid that fact from no one. The shop she owned had a sign inside of a rainbow that read 'Rainbow Friendly.'

Jasmine was a 7 on a scale of 1 to 10. She was a thick woman with a pretty face. She wasn't considered fat because she still had curves. Most men she dated wanted her strictly for her money. Because of that, she had stopped dating men for a while and went strictly female.

Jasmine felt forced into bisexuality by the lack of dating choices for a black woman. At first, she resented her same sex choice. But after her second same sex relationship she was again comfortable in her own skin. Same sex was now her preferred norm. Jasmine felt as though she deserved a 100% Mr. Right. Mainly because she had no children and lots of money. She wasn't rich, but she was very well off.

Jasmine wore her extra pounds as a badge of honor. Jasmine hid behind her bisexual banner to mask her fear of getting hurt. Every item in Jasmines home had a proper name on it. Even her pots and pans were William Sonoma. Jasmine often went on cruises. She'd take Tasha with her and pay for both tickets. Jasmine would babysit for Tasha on occasion. Jasmine would weave Tasha's hair for free. But Tasha had to buy the hair first. Jasmine was one of the few black women Dennis knew who didn't have children.

Tasha had been telling Jasmine about Dennis for months. Tasha was uncomfortable with Jasmine's bisexuality. Tasha had known Jasmine when she was slightly bi curious. Tasha felt Jasmine just needed a good man in her life. Dennis was introduced to Jasmine by Tasha at Jasmines hair salon. Jasmine really didn't have time to speak to Dennis at the time. She was working on two heads at the same time. Jasmine didn't mess around when she was at work. She had to give Dennis the brush off. Tasha had caught Jasmine off guard. But they did exchange numbers.

Catherine hated Tasha as much as she hated Dana. Catherine was jealous of any woman in

Dennis' life, including his mother Florence and
their daughter Princess.
Catherine had driven a permanent wedge between
Dennis and his mother, Florence. Dennis had
stopped calling his mother mom and started
referring to her as Flo. Florence had started calling
Catherine "Cathy." Florence did all she could to
stay relevant in Princess's life. Even if that meant
throwing her only son Dennis under the bus.

Catherine had Florence wrapped around her
finger. Dennis wondered if his mother would be on
her side in the court battle to come. Dana had never
met Jasmine. Even though their aunt Daphne got
her hair styled by Jasmine. Daphne and Jasmine had
a stylist/client relationship only.

Dennis had been hearing Tasha talk about
her single friend Jasmine for almost a year before
they were officially introduced. Dennis preferred to
pick up on women personally. He didn't really go
for 'hook ups' per say. But he only agreed because
Tasha was his close friend and he trusted her
greatly.

This was the first time Tasha had introduced
Dennis to any of her female friends. Dennis called
Jasmine every other night for weeks until they
finally had their first conversation. Jasmine had
immersed herself in her work. Dennis had assumed
she was playing hard to get. But Jasmine wasn't
playing anything. She worked in her shop from
10am to 10pm. She also had 3 other beauticians
renting booths in her shop. Jasmine stayed busy.
Dennis made sure he answered the phone when she
called sporadically. He felt obligated to Tasha to

make an effort to get together with Jasmine. Before Dennis could start in on the Jasmine experience, the therapist stopped him.

The therapist wanted to continue but the time had run out. She told Dennis that they'd pick up here where they left off in next week's session. By the end of this session the therapist was the one who was exhausted instead of Dennis. The therapist had not known of black women who practiced self-loathing on Tasha's level.

The therapist was shocked. Tasha was a lot to take in all at once. The therapist still had to process what she heard for the first time. Dennis was also exhausted as usual after an intense session. Dennis had decided to call in sick for two days. He had court in the morning, and he figured he'd need an extra day for recuperation. He had no papers prepared just child support receipts.

Dennis had decided not to stop by the gym on his way home this time. He wanted to get plenty of rest in anticipation of the stress of court in the morning. Dennis wore his best suit. A navy blue and gold double-breasted suit. He had no lawyer but brought all of his child support receipts.

Catherine had an attorney with her. Since being served with court papers, Dennis hadn't seen his daughter Princess except for 5 minutes at his mother's house. Princess wasn't in the court room. She was at school. Dennis didn't want her there but a small part of him did. He just wanted to see her. Before Catherine unprovokingly removed Princess from Dennis's life, Princess was spending every weekend with her father. Dennis had no idea why he was in court. Catherine was whispering to her attorney.

She wouldn't so much as look in Dennis direction. Catherine's female attorney began accusing Dennis of not taking an active role in his daughter's life. Even though Catherine was purposely keeping Princess from seeing Dennis. Her attorney pointed out that Dennis had time to see a therapist regularly and to have an active social life. Catherine's lawyer was getting her info straight from Catherine.

Catherine got her info straight form Florence. Florence, Tasha and Dana are the only people he trusted enough to tell about the therapist. Dennis felt as powerless as General Custard who had just wandered into an ambush. His mind became temporally dysfunctional due to his blinding anger.

Dennis felt betrayed by his mother Florence. He could barely keep up with or obey the judge's commands. Catherine's lawyer made the judge believe that Dennis chose not to see his daughter anymore. Not mentioning of the fact that Catherine had just stopped bringing Princess over. Even though Dennis continued to pay child support.

The Lawyer had the judge believing Catherine's lies. Catherine had recently broken up with her live-in boyfriend. When her boyfriend left, he took his ample salary with him. Catherine had grown accustomed to a two-income household lifestyle. Dennis had no prior knowledge of their break-up. The lawyer had let it slip. Dennis figured his mother must have known.

I'm Leaving You For A White Woman

The judge awarded Catherine 200 extra dollars a month on top of the 400 she was already receiving. Now his monthly payments were 600. The judge actually ordered Dennis to spend more time with his daughter. The judge said that there was no excuse why Dennis had gone six weeks without seeing his daughter. Dennis screamed out that Catherine wouldn't let him see her. He said that every time he tried to pick her up that she would leave before he got here. The judge didn't believe him. The judge referred to this rebuttal as a cop out. The 400 Dennis was paying wasn't court ordered. It was a suitable amount that Catherine and Dennis had agreed upon. Now Dennis was court ordered to pay 200 extra dollars.

The raise didn't affect Dennis nearly as much as the withholding the visitation of his daughter Princess. Not seeing Princess had taken its toll on Dennis. He was in constant sorrow everyday he went without seeing or hearing from Princess. Days felt like years. The judge granted Catherine more money and sole guardianship giving Dennis every other weekend. So, he lost two weekends per month along with 200 dollars.

Catherine played the perfect victim. Dennis displayed his child support receipts to the judge for naught. Dennis waited a few minutes in court after Catherine left with her lawyer. He was afraid to run into Catherine in the elevator. Dennis left court and went straight to his mother's house.

As he pulled up, he saw Catherine's car parked out front. Dennis sat in his car for 10 minutes before driving off. He just didn't have anything left in him. Dennis bypassed the gym and drove straight home. He was so depressed, he turned his phone off and just laid in the bed.

Dennis clutched his picture of Princess as the tears streamed down his face. He felt he had no one. Thoughts of suicide ran back and forth across his mind. His next therapy session was in 3 more days. Dennis doubted if he could make it that long.

Good thing he took off two days. Because he was in no condition to return to work. Dennis went to sleep. He only slept 3 hours. He was awakened with the thought of seeing his daughter in a week. Now he had a court order to back him up. If Catherine played any more games, Dennis had paperwork for protection.

Dennis checked his phone and saw he had missed 2 calls. One from his mother and one from La Ronda. Dennis had initially decided not to date La Ronda. He personally felt she was just too naive for him. Dennis also didn't like how much her parents controlled her. But at that moment coming out of depression, naive was just what the doctor ordered.

Dennis felt he needed a warm bath. He spoke to La Ronda while in the tub. He put his phone on speaker then placed it on the sink. La Ronda's childlike persona was like music to Dennis's soul. This was the first time he had smiled in a week. La Ronda had brought laughter back into Dennis. La Ronda and Dennis spoke until his bath water turned cold.

Since Dennis had already taken the next day off, he figured why spend it alone. Plus, he figured he'd have more to talk to his therapist about. Dennis suggested a one-day cruise to Catalina Island. La Ronda became immediately ecstatic just from the idea.

After talking to La Ronda, Dennis felt strong enough to return his mother's call. Dennis figured Catherine had briefed Florence on the day's events. Catherine confided in Florence more than her own mother. Catherine's mother hated Dennis as much as Catherine did. Catherine's mother had only been fed one side of the story. Dennis felt the deck was unfairly stacked in her favor. The judge, lawyer, Florence and Catherine's mother.

Florence, however, didn't mention the days courtroom drama. But from the evasive tone of her voice, Dennis knew Catherine had already told her. Of course, Florence would only believe Catherine's version anyway. Dennis figured telling her would be a moot point. Florence had told Dennis that Catherine had just left and she didn't have the baby with her. Catherine had Florence so brainwashed that Florence was scared to call Dennis when she was there.

Dennis found it angrily pathetic on Florence's part. Especially since Catherine never liked Florence herself. Now they're so-called best friends, united by a common enemy, Dennis. Florence was doing all she could to talk Dennis into coming over. She had some errands she wanted to run, and she didn't want to drive alone. Dennis told his mother that he'd be by for breakfast Saturday.

That was his way of saying no hard feelings. No matter what, Dennis still loved his mom a great deal. He knew her betrayal was motivated by her love for her granddaughter and her fear of being cut out of her life. But it still hurt Dennis deeply.

Chapter 6

After hanging up, Dennis called La Ronda. He had surprisingly had a great conversation with her that left him wanting more. He and La Ronda spoke all night. The conversation stayed light. They finally finished talking close to 10pm. Dennis went to bed blocking Catherine's activities from his mind.

He was trying to concentrate on La Ronda. Nevertheless, it was Catherine who consumed his thoughts. Dennis was growing to develop a festered hatred for the woman he once was engaged to. Since Dennis knew La Ronda had a parental curfew, he picked La Ronda up early. Her parents were both at work.

Dennis felt a sigh of relief. He didn't have to be subjected to another interview by her father. La Ronda gave him a big kiss and hug on the front porch. Dennis felt so happy with La Ronda. Dennis and La Ronda went on their date heading to Long

Beach. That's where the ship was docked. Dennis found La Ronda beautifully strange. She had the conversation of a junior high school student. Her lack of social experience made Dennis feel powerful.

La Ronda had packed a small suitcase just as Dennis had instructed her to. Dennis took his change of clothes and stuffed them into La Ronda's suitcase. They boarded the vessel as scheduled. La Ronda had never been to Catalina Island. She had never been anywhere.

This was Dennis second time on a ship. He and gone on a 4-day cruise with Catherine many years ago. They put the one suitcase in the room and went on a brief tour of the ship. They both found themselves on the upper deck. Dennis was drinking a complimentary whiskey sour. La Ronda was drinking a root beer float. La Ronda had frowned when Dennis ordered his alcoholic beverage. La Ronda didn't smoke or drink. Nevertheless, Dennis was enjoying hanging out with her.

Every time Dennis went to initiate physical contact between the two of them, La Ronda would shy away. Dennis didn't mind too much. He could sense himself entering "The Friend Zone." Dennis didn't want to be in La Ronda's friend zone. He was physically attracted to La Ronda and he wanted to be her boyfriend and possibly more.

La Ronda wasn't shy by no means. She had introduced herself to most of the staff as she and Dennis walked past them when the ship docked in Catalina for two hours.

I'm Leaving You For A White Woman

Dennis and La Ronda rented a golf cart and went to dinner. They enjoyed their meal twice as much as each other's company. Dennis could tell that La Ronda was a tad bit uncomfortable.

After eating, Dennis and La Ronda bought a few souvenirs then boarded the ship. Once off the ship, they both took separate showers and changed into appropriate dinner attire. They went to dinner arm and arm. Dennis could feel that La Ronda wasn't as attracted to him as he was to her. But in the face of the public La Ronda acted as such.

Dennis was satisfied with that. The both of them enjoyed their entire day together. On the way home, La Ronda had complained how late it was. Right before they pulled up at La Ronda's house, she kissed Dennis on his left cheek. Dennis drove home frustrated over the lack of romantic physical contact between himself and La Ronda. He could tell she liked him but not in the way he wanted.

Dennis went home and called Tasha. He told her he was not going to let Catherine bring him down. He felt he was back on his way onto the dating scene again. Tasha was always a good ear for Dennis. Sometimes he called her just to vent. He always asked either Tasha or his sister Dana when questions about women arose.

Dennis was willing to take it slow with La Ronda. That's because he blamed his past relationships failures on moving too fast. Tasha felt Dennis was lucky to have La Ronda. But Dennis knew Tasha's reasons. Tasha liked the fact that La Ronda's parents were so involved.

Their parental involvement creeped Dennis out. They disagreed on several points but still enjoyed speaking to each other. Their conversations sometimes ended up in the "Who's on First" category.

Dennis mid-terms were all next week. He was planning to catch up on some studying during the up and coming weekend. But before he could begin, he had yet another counseling session. Since Catherine wasn't participating, the counseling sessions became more like individual therapy sessions. Dennis' H.M.O. Insurance covered it leaving only a 10-dollar co-pay.

Friday came, and Dennis was heading to therapy after work. Again, as he arrived at his session his therapist spoke on him joining in and contribution in her group sessions. She wanted Dennis to hear and benefit from some of the other men's stories. Dennis told her he'd think about it. He was eager to tell his therapist how his date went with La Ronda. His therapist wasn't interested. Instead, she wished to elaborate on Tasha and Catherine.

His therapist felt they'd make more progress if they dissected his relationship with his sister, mother, aunt, and baby momma. His therapist opened up with where they'd left off. She had a week to ponder the shocking information that Dennis had given her. She actually used his story about Tasha in her men's group which was largely made up of Black and Latino males.

Dennis, however, didn't want to discuss Tasha. He felt that she wasn't relevant since the two never dated. Minus that one night of passion. Dennis instead began discussing Jasmine. Jasmine was Tasha's friend that he dated that he never dated. It was complicated. Jasmine made at least twice as much money as Dennis but felt threatened by him. Jasmine was a thick heavyset woman. Shapely but by no means fat. During one of their late night 5-minute conversations, Jasmine apologized for being too stand-offish when they met. Jasmine told Dennis that she was very serious when it came to her business. She also told Dennis not to ever come to her beauty shop again unless he was getting a perm.

This was the first time Dennis had dated a friend of Tasha's. Dennis had hooked up Tasha with several of his friends in the past. Nothing ever panned out. Tasha gave reasons that validated their rejection. But Dennis knew the real reason. If they weren't light skinned, bi-racial or White, then she would either self-sabotage the effort or just refuse them all together.

Because Dennis was dark-skinned, he would get offended by Tasha's comments at times. He never told her because she never directed comments towards him. Dennis personally felt everyone has a right to their opinion. He saw Tasha as a real friend. He wouldn't say or do anything that would hurt her feelings. Dennis would use Tasha to vent, but Tasha used Dennis to vent as well.

Dennis had hooked Tasha up with his dentist. He was Tall, semi-muscular and had no children. He drove a convertible BMW, and he had no wife or girlfriend. Dennis had even pre-screened the dentist on two prior visits before he decided to introduce them. The dentist was from Jamaica via New York. He wore his hair short and had a slight accent. Tasha went on two dates with the dentist. Dennis felt she dated him just to please him but had no real interest.

Dennis asked Tasha what happened to the dentist. He seemed to be everything Tasha claimed she needed. Tasha had complained that Mark wasn't helping her at all. She said she wanted a man with no kids who didn't mind if she had one herself. She wanted a handsome man with a good/great job. Tasha told Dennis that the dentist got on her nerves. But she worded her response in a way that Dennis thought otherwise.

She told Dennis she couldn't stand his "bossy black ass." Tasha's sons father Mark is legally married and a great father to his kids by his white wife. Dennis had a problem with that. Dennis had a problem with the fact that through all the drama, Mark still used Tasha as a pop-up booty call. Tasha wouldn't let a black man treat her with such disrespect. Since then, Dennis had stayed out of Tasha's personal life. Especially when it came to Mark.

Dennis felt by staying out of it and keeping his opinions to himself, he'd lengthen the life expectancy of their friendship. Dennis initially liked Jasmine and all that she represented. Dennis would call Jasmine every night after 10pm. That was the only time he would catch her. Dennis preferred a thick black woman as opposed to a thin one. He was extremely attracted to Jasmine.

I'm Leaving You For A White Woman

Jasmine had a set of pouty lips that he was dying to kiss. When it came to Jasmine, Dennis was head over heels. Jasmine did hair weaves all day but wore her own hair short. It looked good to Dennis. Tasha met Jasmine as a hairdresser to client. Over time they became friends.

Jasmine enjoyed talking to Dennis for 5 to 10 minutes a night. It took some time to work up to that. Most nights when Dennis called, Jasmine sounded vague and unresponsive. Most times she gave one-word answers. Dennis was the main conversationalist between the two of them to say the least.

Dennis did all he could to date or hook up with Jasmine. Jasmine would call Dennis once or twice a week. It was always during her lunch break. Jasmine only took a 30-minute lunch break between 12pm to 12:30 pm even thought she was the boss. Jasmine was extremely disciplined when it came to her shop. Dennis found her work ethic attractive. Dennis however did wish that Jasmine would contribute more to the conversations. When she would call him at lunch, she'd be more talkative than when she was at night.

Dennis thought nothing of it. They both took lunch at noon. Dennis could never spend lunch with Jasmine. Her shop was too far away from the school where he worked. So, after accepting Jasmines offer, he called his mom. He wanted to let his mother know in advance, so she wouldn't worry. Florence didn't mind. She told Dennis that she had planned to go to breakfast with Cathy and the baby. Dennis knew his mother was lying.

Florence said that only to hurt him. Dennis paid her no mind. By now Dennis was use to his mother and her passive aggressiveness and guilt mongering that she used as a defense mechanism. Dennis got off of the phone as fast as he could. Brunch was perfect for Dennis. He had to pick up Princess Saturday night. Princes was only 4yrs old at the time. Jasmine insisted on picking Dennis up. This was a strange twist for Dennis. On most of his dates he did the driving.

When Jasmine pulled up, she didn't get out of the car. She texted Dennis from the car that she was downstairs. Dennis had seen Jasmine pull up from the window. She spoke on her cell phone to someone else for nearly 10 minutes in his driveway before she texted Dennis.

Dennis was dressed and ready to go. As he walked downstairs, Jasmine hung up the phone and unlocked Dennis's door. As soon as Dennis got into the car, Jasmine leaned over and kissed him. A quick peck on the lips. This satisfied Dennis' need to know. He couldn't get a real vibe on Jasmine because of the short but frequent phone calls. Just that little kiss was all that was needed to put Dennis at ease. He felt that her interest was beyond platonic.

Jasmine was quite the talker. This was their first date, but they had been corresponding by telephone for close to two weeks. Jasmine actually did most of the talking. Dennis was amazed at how much Jasmine could eat. Her appetite turned Dennis on. He was sort of turned off by her conversation primarily consisting of hair.

Jasmine was about her money. Dennis didn't have a problem with Jasmine's weight. But Jasmine did. Jasmine kept making insulting comments about herself referring to her weight. She was commenting while she was eating. Dennis kept complementing her on her looks. He wasn't patronizing her. That was truly how he felt. Every time he complimented Jasmine she smiled. He knew what he was saying was seeping through.

Dennis paid for the meal. He insisted, that's just the way he was raised. Jasmine kept offering, nay insisting if you will about dessert and its importance. Dennis was at a loss for words. He was so caught up in the moment, he didn't give it much thought. Besides he hadn't eaten breakfast, so he took several liberties at the buffet bar.

Jasmine was not only talkative, she had taken the lead in the conversation. Dennis had gotten that little tingling feeling. He was thinking Jasmine was the one. Besides, Dennis had complained to Tasha that he didn't have time for a needy woman. He had vented one night that he wanted to date a more independent woman. So, Tasha introduced him to a woman that seemed to compliment his rant.

Jasmine stood up and excused herself to the ladies' room. Dennis stood up as Jasmine stood up. Then he sat back down. This was the happiest Dennis had been in a long time. He continued eating his food. Dennis had mistakenly picked up his egg's benedict like a fried breakfast sandwich. But an eggs benedict is not a fried egg sandwich. So when

Dennis bit into it, the over easy egg yolk had burst and squirted all over Dennis new suit.

When Jasmine returned from the restroom, she saw the yolk stain, and both began to laugh. When their eyes met, shared expressions mutually decided it was time to leave. As they drove away, Dennis noticed that they were going the opposite way from whence they came. But he was game and just going with the flow. Jasmine referred again to desert.

Dennis was pretty stuffed. Dennis and Jasmine didn't order dessert at the restaurant. So for them to drive to a totally new restaurant or bakery for dessert, Dennis assumed that this place must specialize in pastries. Much to his surprise, they pulled up to valet parking at a hotel. Jasmine took Dennis by the hand to the elevator. Jasmine had taken Dennis to a suite she had rented before she picked Dennis up. When they walked in, Dennis was stunned.

He didn't see this coming in a million years. Jasmine had rose pedals and chocolates neatly placed all over the room. Jasmine held out her arms for a hug. Then she asked Dennis was he ready for dessert. Dennis said "Yes" as she went into the restroom

Jasmine emerged 5 minutes later dressed in red lingerie matching the rose pedals. She laid Dennis on his back on the bed, handcuffed him, and began to strip him. Jasmine covered Dennis in whipped cream only to lick it off while she fed him chocolates. Jasmine made love to Dennis for an hour. Dennis was handcuffed the entire time.

Jasmine and Dennis date ended when she dropped him off at home close to 6pm. That left Dennis plenty of time to pick up Princess from Catherine's house. Running a tad bit behind schedule, Dennis decided not to change his clothes. Instead he went straight to his car to pick up Princess.

This posed a problem. Catherine had a 6 o'clock class and Dennis was supposed to be there no later than 5:15pm. When he pulled up at 6:10pm Catherine came busting out of the house mouth first. She was cursing and going off on Dennis while he was trying to apologize for his tardiness. Catherine couldn't hear him over the sound of her own voice. Now Catherine had claimed that since he was late, he couldn't pick up Princess. She said that Princess was at her mom's house.

Dennis knew that was all a fabricated rouse because he could see her in the window. The only reason Catherine had given Dennis the weekends is because she had a Saturday class. Catherine changed the co-parenting drop off and pick up schedule according to the convenience of her life. Dennis had to be ready for almost anything.

Most of the time during Catherine's rants, Dennis would just shake his head and ignore her. On this particular evening he wasn't able to keep his cool. Catherine was attempting to teach Dennis a lesson. She had it in her head to play with his visitations based on her emotions.

Catherine was cruelly punitive. While Dennis and Catherine were arguing, the police had pulled up. Dennis went to explain to the officers what had happened. The police officers walked past him and started speaking to Catherine. The police then put Dennis in handcuffs and placed him in the back of the squad car.

Dennis had nothing to fear. He hadn't touched her nor made a verbal threat. He sat in the car for 20 minutes before the officers came back to the car to ask for Dennis side of the story. After the police took Dennis's statement, they booked him on the suspicion of Domestic Violence.

Dennis was arrested, and his car was impounded. Dennis was trying to explain to the police that he never touched her. The arresting officers excuse was O.J. Simpson. They told Dennis that since the O.J. Simpson case, whenever they receive a domestic violence call that someone had to go to jail.

Dennis was booked into the county jail. This was his first time he was ever in handcuff's let alone jail. He was placed in a holding cell still wearing his stained suit. Inside the holding cell he witnessed two fights over gang beefs. This world Dennis knew nothing of.

He was then called out of the cell to get his new inmate attire. He was held on 35,000 dollars bail. He called his mother and she put up 3,500 for his bail. As soon as Dennis got out of jail, he went to get his car out of impound. He was in jail for 45 days until his mother could scrape the money together. When he went to get his car out of impound it took every dime he had. While he was in jail, Catherine created a paper trail to show him missing his weekends.

She purposely didn't mention in the report that Dennis couldn't see his daughter because he was in jail. She had it written up as if it was his choice to abandon his parental duty. When Dennis went back to court, he was sentenced to time served and 52 weeks of domestic violence classes. Each class costing 25 dollars per week.

Dennis had called Jasmine after almost 2 months, but he didn't tell her where he was. If she knew where he was then she'd ask for what? Dennis didn't want her to actually think that he was a batterer.

Jasmine saw the near two-month absence of Dennis differently. From her point of view, she had sex with him and then didn't hear from him again. Dennis had no acceptable reason to offer Jasmine. She felt used and thrown away. She wanted nothing to do with Dennis anymore. This was the last time Dennis spoke to Jasmine.

This made Dennis even angrier at Catherine. He blamed her for the entire ordeal. Dennis didn't date anyone during his 52-week classes, but he kept contact with La Ronda. He had sunk into a misogynistic depression. During this period, he began drinking heavily. Catherine had filed for sole custody while Dennis was in jail. All the judge had to see was that Dennis was behind bars for domestic violence. He ruled in Catherine's favor within 10 minutes.

That particular change ruined his chance for going to Pro. He was subsequently kicked off of the semi-pro team he was on. He had just a few months to go until he would be eligible for a walk-on trial for the NBA. He was actually ordered "removed from the league because of the domestic violence charge." That prevented Dennis from being picked up by another team.

Dennis finished his domestic violence classes in one year. Then for the next few years he worked on getting his record expunged. It was a long way back for Dennis. The only place Dennis was able to find a job was at the high school he once attended. He held several basketball records for his alma matter. This particular therapy session was a bit heavy for Dennis.

He considered Jasmine as the one who got away. The stirring up of that inside made him ever angrier. He thought about how long he had been at the mercy of Catherine's attitude. Dennis despised the way Catherine used Princess like a hostage and child support like ransom. He hated the fact that his mother knew this and did nothing. Not only did she not do anything on Dennis's behalf. She teamed up on the side of Catherine so she could have overnight visitation with Princess.

Now Dennis was in a situation where he was actually competing against his mother for time with his daughter. The close relationship between Catherine and Dennis' mother Florence, warped his relationship with his own mother. He didn't know whether to love or hate her.

The more Florence treated Catherine like a daughter, the more Catherine and Dennis developed a brother and sister relationship. Thus, making the idea of reconciliation between Dennis and Catherine feel incestuous.

Dennis couldn't help thinking Florence was orchestrating this passive aggressively by design. Dennis had started referring to child support as ransom. He had started to refer to his daughter as kidnapped. Dennis' hatred for Catherine and Florence grew then festered into unbearable disdain. The hatred of Florence started a conflict within himself in direct opposition with his love for her.

Somehow the conflict between the two extreme feelings created the guilt he feels. Thus, warping his perception of all he sees, hears, and feels from the opposite sex. Dennis left his therapy session totally drained again. This time was slightly different. Stirring up old feelings over Jasmine, had Dennis feeling regret. He had all but forgotten about Jasmine. To whom he referred to as "The One That Got Away." He knew better than to go up to her shop. Drop in visits were her pet peeve. Even though he decided to drive up there anyways.

He was driving to the flower shop with hopes of forgiveness and a possible second chance. He stopped at the florist on his way to her shop. He purchased a dozen roses. Discussing her in such detail dug up unresolved feelings about Jasmine. When Dennis pulled up, he was disappointed to see her shop was no longer there. Apparently, she had moved a while ago. The new tenants had no recollection of her every being there.

Dennis called Tasha on the way home. He wanted Jasmine's new information. Tasha was shocked that Dennis even remembered her. This was Tasha's first time hearing her name in years. Tasha told Dennis that Jasmine had her stopped

speaking when Dennis stopped talking to her.
Tasha knew Dennis was in jail. She didn't know if
Jasmine knew or not. Because of that, she stayed
out of it. Because of Jasmine's size and bank
account she was no stranger to getting used and
discarded by men.

Dennis told Tasha that the first and only date
with Jasmine was the best date he ever had. He
could tell Jasmine liked him too. Dennis hadn't
thought of Jasmine in over a year. Looking for her
at her previous shop location was a long shot at
best. Tasha had asked Dennis was he going to his
Aunts Daphne's party?

Dennis knew nothing about it. Tasha
informed Dennis that his aunt Daphne sent out E-
mail invitations. Dennis drove home to check his e-
mails. There he found his invitation. His aunt
Daphne threw a lot of parties. They didn't have to
have a theme necessarily. She loved dinner parties
and alcohol.

Dennis first mind was to invite La Ronda.
He figured why invite Tasha she has her own
invitation. Before actually calling La Ronda he first
called Tasha. Dennis needed advice so he called his
sister Dana. He knew Dana and her man Derek
would be there. Dana never turned down a meal.

Dennis asked her advice on whether or not
he should invite La Ronda. Dennis didn't want to do
too much too soon. Dennis figured it might be too
early to introduce La Ronda to his family. He knew
his mother and aunt could be a bit much at times.
But Denis didn't want to show up alone. And he
didn't want to rush the gun with La Ronda.

I'm Leaving You For A White Woman

When he explained his dilemma to Dana, she told him to go ahead and bring her. Dana told Dennis that he couldn't hide her from his family forever. They both shared a laugh and Dennis agreed to bring La Ronda to the get together.

It suddenly dawned on Dennis that he hadn't called La Ronda yet. Dennis called La Ronda but got no answer. So he left a message about the get together. He stayed by his phone waiting for her to call. Dennis was so exhausted. He fell asleep. When Dennis woke up, he saw that La Ronda had called.

La Ronda left him a message saying that she'd love to go. But first she'd have to check with her parents. Every time she said that to Dennis it would spark a minor debate. Dennis couldn't digest the fact that La Ronda was in her thirties and still had to check with her parents over every little thing. Dennis did all he could to keep his opinions to himself.

This would give Dennis a second look at La Ronda. Dennis wanted to know if it's his company she liked so much or the date and location of that first date. This date wouldn't be so extravagant. It would be a basic get together with family and friends. Even though Dennis wanted to take it slow with La Ronda, a small part of him wanted to turn up the heat.

The Alexander women had a reputation of judgmental practices when it came to the mates of their children, male or female. Dennis knew this was inevitable, so he might as well get it over with. Dennis knew his mother may or may not be there.

He knew if there's alcohol and family there then
there will be gambling. Dennis's mother and aunt
always played spades at functions. It was sort of a
tradition. Usually at Daphne's parties its more
women there than men.

Dennis usually showed up alone and ended
up siting with Derek on the front porch sharing a
bottle of Cognac. That's because Dennis ofttimes
didn't bring a date. The last few functions Dennis
had been showing up alone. This would be Dennis's
way of showing his family members that they need
not be concerned. His family knew about him and
the therapist. It was supposed to be couple's
counseling

Since Catherine and Dennis had agreed not
to reconcile then couples counseling seemed
unnecessary. Dennis went by the next morning to
pick up La Ronda. Dennis still had the box of roses
from a day prior. He took the card off of the box
addressed to Jasmine and put it in a trash can in
front of La Ronda's neighbor's house. He
approached the door with a box filled with a dozen
roses.

Dennis figured the roses were already paid
for. No need letting them go to waste. Besides they
were still gift wrapped. La Ronda's mother
answered the door and gave the biggest smile when
she saw the flowers. Dennis's gentle nature fit well
with La Ronda's sheltered upbringing.

Her parents seemed to approve of Dennis
dating their daughter. This was very important to La
Ronda. La Ronda had a history of bringing the
wrong guy home. So far Dennis was scoring points.

I'm Leaving You For A White Woman

La Ronda loved the flowers. La Ronda and Dennis left headed to his aunt's house. Dennis was nervous because this was the first time Dennis had introduced a woman to his family since Catherine. Dennis and La Ronda weren't at that stage in their relationship. But sometimes the best way to know how well you can swim is to dive into the deep end.

Dennis stopped at the grocery store on the way to his aunts and picked up two bottles of wine. One white and one red. La Ronda saw what Dennis had purchased and made small insignificant comments of disapproval about his choice of beverage. Dennis ignored her and bought an additional bottle. Dennis chose a dry champagne. La Ronda started complaining about the alcohol all of the way to Dennis' aunt Daphne's house.

Dennis and La Ronda pulled up and entered. La Ronda was dressed well with her long flowing curly hair down her back. She usually wore her hair up in a teacher's style bun. Dennis was pleased with how she looked. Dennis felt safe and secure whenever the two of them were together.

A lot of it was due to La Ronda's sheltered upbringing and arrested development. Her damsel in destress demeanor fit well with his current deflated ego and sense of self-worth. La Ronda stopped at all doors and waited until Dennis opened them. No matter how far back he was. This was to let him know how and what treatment she was accustomed to.

As soon as they walked, in all eyes were on them. Dennis walked over to the kitchen to get his aunt. Daphne came out and introduced herself to La

Ronda first. Then Daphne introduced everyone in attendance; Tasha, Dennis' friend, Eddie Dennis's best friend, Dana Dennis's sister, Derek Dana's husband, Florence Dennis' mother.

Derek had invited two men from his job Byron and Clifford. Catherine was there, she had been invited by Florence. Tasha had found and convinced Jasmine to come. This was Tasha's surprise and gift to Dennis. No anyone including Tasha knew that Dennis was bringing La Ronda. No one even knew Dennis was dating anyone.

Jasmine smiled condescendingly at Tasha. As if Tasha purposely invited Jasmine to humiliate her. Before Dennis got there, Tasha was concerned whether or not Catherine would be a problem. This was a big slap in the face in a multitude of ways. Dennis was slightly relieved when he saw that Princess wasn't there. Dennis just froze like a deer caught in headlights when he saw Jasmine

It had been over a year since Dennis had seen Jasmine. She was still pretty. Her hair was past her shoulders. Jasmine had put in a fresh weave. She had more than reasonable amount of jewelry of her fingers, wrist and around her neck. Tasha took Dennis by the wrist and pulled him into the back yard.

La Ronda had sat down on the sectional sofa. Derek had sat next to her and tried to create small talk with La Ronda. That was mainly to distract her. La Ronda looked bewildered as if she was attempting to process what was taking place. Tasha and Dennis had begun to discuss the best way to handle this situation.

Dennis felt responsible because he didn't tell anyone he was bringing someone. Tasha said she would take Jasmine with her and leave. The only reason Jasmine came was because Tasha begged her to. Tasha had explained to Jasmine that Dennis had gone to jail. She told Jasmine everything that Dennis had told her about Jasmine just two days prior. He wasn't thinking about Jasmine until he brought her up during his last session.

When Tasha and Dennis walked back inside, the demographics of the party had changed. La Ronda got upset when Tasha took Dennis by the hand and went into the back yard. She had assumed Tasha was his baby momma because of their perceived familiarity. She struck up a conversation with Byron, who was a friend of Derek's. Byron and La Ronda left together to go on a beer run.

Jasmine stayed purposely so she could confront Dennis and La Ronda at the same time. Dennis was seeing red. He couldn't truly see how pissed off Jasmine was because he was so angry at Florence for bringing Catherine. Dennis walked right past Jasmine and began asking Florence why did she bring Catherine? Florence was hanging on the idea of Dennis, Princess and Catherine becoming a family one day.

Dennis was just in court last week. He felt that he had been treated prodigiously unfair. Catherine had taken advantage of a system that took advantage of Dennis. Innocently unaware, Florence played right into Catherine's plan to destroy Dennis for having the audacity to attempt to be happy without her.

Daphne claimed not to be "In it," as she puts it. But Daphne backs anything her sister Florence supports. There were a few people there that Dennis didn't know. Daphne was bitterly divorced. She would often join in as a willing participant in the pathetic cesspool of self-pity with Florence and Catherine.

Dana was Dennis's ally or the closest thing to an ally along with Tasha. No one was paying attention to Jasmine, and Jasmine was known as an exhibitionist. She was being as patient as she could while she was drinking wine glass after glass. Derek, Dana's common law husband was talking to Jasmine while the two of them were drinking.

Byron walked in with a giggling La Ronda. Dennis had just been introduced to Byron less than 20 minutes ago. Now in walks Byron with a Kool-Aid smile wearing La Ronda. When Dennis walked away with Tasha, Byron assumed Tasha was Dennis's baby momma also. So, Byron took it upon himself to speak to La Ronda.

Byron and La Ronda had looks on their faces that spoke volumes. La Ronda had a naïve child-like air to herself that men found irresistibly enticing. Jasmine, who was now intoxicated began in on Tasha. Tasha had done quite a bit of sweet talking and begging on behalf of Dennis to get Jasmine to attend a party where she knew no one.

Jasmine started talking with her hands and neck rolling and spewing obscenities as if she didn't notice or care that Florence and Daphne were seniors in their late 50's and early 60's. Jasmine, who apparently couldn't hold her liquor, directed her anger first at Tasha. Then it went to Dennis. La Ronda was in shock at the whole scene. Jasmine was cursing at Dennis while La Ronda was pulling Dennis by the arm motioning to leave. Dennis was looking for help in the faces of Derek and Dana. Derek was basically hen pecked

In Derek and Dana's household, it was Dana who was the bread winner and pants wearer between the two of them. Jasmine in her embarrassing drunken rant said to Tasha "And where are those roses? You said this fool bought me a dozen roses. I guess that was a lie too."

Dennis looked right in the shocked disappointed face of La Ronda. Just then, La Ronda's eyes swell up with tears realizing that Dennis gave her another woman's flowers. She was so embarrassed, she ran to the restroom and locked the door. Everyone could hear her crying but had no idea why. No one knew about the flowers but Tasha, Jasmine, Dennis and La Ronda

Tasha took as much verbal abuse she could from a drunk Jasmine before she snapped and started cursing back. Tasha and Jasmine were now in the face of one another screaming profanities at one another. Jasmine slapped Tasha and the two began fist fighting right in Daphne's living room. The two women ended up crashing into the dining room table knocking the food onto the floor spilling several bottles of wine on Daphne's shag carpeting.

La Ronda was scared to come out of the restroom. She had never witnessed a scene like that. These educated professional women went from bourgeois to ghetto in 60 seconds.

Derek, Dennis and Derek's friend Clifford were working feverishly to separate the two women who were fighting like two alley cats. Chunks of hair weave struck the wine-soaked carpet. Guest weren't leaving as expected. Quite the contrary. The fight seemed to spark the stunned group of party goers to offer helpful hints and advice all at once.

When the women were separated, Tasha was dragged away to the guest room. Jasmine was too drunk to responsibly drive herself home. Derek's friend Byron offered to drive Jasmine home. In an instant, La Ronda emerged from the restroom. She had washed off her make-up and her head was down. La Ronda walled up to Byron and asked could he take her home. Dennis spoke up before Byron could answer and said, "I'll take her home." La Ronda rolled her eyes and said "I'd rather walk" right in Dennis face. Dennis didn't wish to argue. He felt responsible so he stayed behind to help clean up.

Clifford and Derek left together. Dana and Tasha stayed to clean up. That's when Dennis overheard Catherine in Daphne's bedroom talking to Florence. Catherine was venomously expressing her concern for Princess safety in Dennis presence. Florence didn't respond, although she listened attentively. Dennis was just too tired to comment. He pretended not to hear them. He made eye-piercing contact with Tasha then walked her to her car.

Tasha and Dennis were leaning against her car as they discussed what had just transpired. Dennis's love for his friendship with Tasha out weighted his shock and anger of the evening. Dennis approached the subject straight forward, yet delicately.

"Tasha, what made you tell her about the flowers? Why didn't you tell me she was coming?" asked Dennis politely as he could.

"You were damn near stalking the woman when you called me "answered Tasha.

"I wasn't stalking anyone"

"Yes you were! You were driving up to her hair salon."

"She was just on my mind because my therapist made me bring her up."

"And then you show up with that high yellow chick."

"What does that have to do with anything?" asked Dennis in all inquisitive tone.

"Come on Dennis, don't play dumb. I mean you walked in with that pretty light skinned girl with all that long ass good hair and Jasmine standing over there, fat and damn near bald headed under her weave."

Dennis just shook his head. He knew how Tasha was and just accepted it. He knew La Ronda was drop dead gorgeous by most standards.

A small part of Dennis wanted Catherine to see him with a beautiful happy woman on his arm. In recent weeks Dennis was hit hard in court. He didn't have the backing of Florence or Daphne. He figured his mother might invite Catherine and she did.

Tasha got in her car and left. When Dennis walked to his car, he saw that someone had flattened two of his tires. Someone had keyed the word "asshole" on the hood of his car. Dennis knew that it was Jasmine or La Ronda. Dennis had to go back in the house with Dana, Clifford, Derek, Daphne, Florence and Catherine.

Tasha had long since driven off. Dennis had to walk back into Daphne's house. The room became instantly eerily silent. Dennis couldn't hold his head up inside the house. He was embarrassed mainly because Catherine was still there. Daphne went in on Dennis calling him everything other than his name.

Daphne was Dennis's favorite aunt. He had the utmost respect for her. When Florence was battling cancer, it was Daphne who took care of Dana and Dennis until she came home from the hospital. Florence fell ill 6 months after the death of Dennis' father. Dennis looked upon Daphne as a second mother.

Dennis had asked Dana for a ride home. When Dana asked why, Dennis had to explain what had happened to his car. Catherine laughed, shook

her head and left. Florence went to get her purse
and left with Catherine, the person she came with.
Dennis offered to have Daphne's carpet cleaned.
Aunt Daphne informed Dennis that she was
replacing the carpet and she would send Dennis the
bill. Everyone left one after the other. Dennis,
Derek and Dana took one last look at Dennis's car
before taking him home.

He was surprised that La Ronda didn't call
him. He reported his car to his insurance company
as vandalized after paying a 500-dollar deductible.
His car was towed to be repaired.

Chapter 7

Dennis was looking forward to keeping his daughter next weekend. That seemed to be his only source of refuge, release and happiness. Dennis attempted to get in contact with La Ronda on several occasions. She would just hang up in his face. He knew how sensitive and childlike La Ronda was. Even so, he still wanted to be with her. Dennis figured he'd give her a few days. This was the first disagreement he and La Ronda ever had.

He was so angry at himself over the flowers. He was beating himself up for being so cheap. La Ronda meant much more to him than a recycled gift. He pondered ways to make it up to her.

Over the next few days, Dennis grew tired of La Ronda answering the phone, letting him speak then hanging up. Dennis decided to go over to La Ronda's house. This was his first time coming over without calling.

He knew her parents would be angry, but he was willing to take anything her mom or dad would dish out. As Dennis was driving, he was thinking of any excuse to keep from actually going over to La Ronda's house. The closer he got, the stronger the butterflies in his stomach fluttered.

He stopped off at the florist and bought one white rose. This was his way of saying how special she was to him. Dennis had fallen in love with La Ronda without being aware of it. He had grown fond of those late-night calls and puzzling conversations. She had replaced Tasha as his favorite person to talk to,

As soon as he pulled up, he decided that he would make his feelings known. He realized her naïve nature made him feel as if he was back in high school dating the star cheerleader. Dennis approached the door with rose in hand. He rang the doorbell and Dennis was surprised to see that La Ronda had answered the door. This was the first time La Ronda had answered the door. Usually her mother or father answered it.

La Ronda's eyes nearly jumped out of her head when she saw Dennis.

"What are you doing here? You have to go." Whispered La Ronda.

"Baby I messed up. I'm so sorry" Dennis said in an apologetic voice as he handed La Ronda the single rose. "I would like to speak to your father" said Dennis. He knew La Ronda told her parents everything. He knew she was totally guided by them. La Ronda replied "My parents are on vacation. They won't be back for another week. So you really need to just go." Dennis just then noticed that La Ronda was wearing a Japanese Kimono and it was 5pm. When La Ronda said her parents were on vacation, Dennis figured this would be the best time to get down on bended knee and make his heart-felt plea.

Dennis pushed open the door, at that exact same moment La Ronda muttered "I have company." Dennis was face to face with another man in his boxers. He didn't remember the guy's name, but he looked familiar. It was Byron, Derek's friend from Dennis' aunts party. Dennis flew into a jealous rage. He felt Byron was in violation. He was just at Dennis's aunt's house. Now he was having sex with Dennis's girlfriend La Ronda. What added injury to insult, Dennis and La Ronda hadn't been intimate with each other in a while. Dennis was trying to take it slow with her.

The introduction of La Ronda to Dennis' family ended in disaster before it started, now this. Dennis punched Byron in the face. But Dennis was a teacher, not a fighter. Byron punched Dennis several times in the stomach and face. As Dennis went crashing to the floor, La Ronda was ending her 911 call. Dennis made it to his feet and attempted one more punch. Byron leaned back letting Dennis miss a looping right-hand lead. Byron then punched him into La Ronda's glass end table, shattering it.

The police arrive to find a badly cut Dennis Alexander picking shards of glass out of his arms and legs.

"Who lives here?" asked the Senior officer.

La Ronda answered "I do. This guy burst through the door and attacked my boyfriend."

With La Ronda naming Dennis as the aggressive outside agitator. and Byron as her boyfriend, the police arrested Dennis.

As the police were putting Dennis in handcuffs, La Ronda ran up to Dennis and said while chuckling "You forgot your flower" as she stuck what was left of his white rose in his pocket. The Senior officer felt sorry for Dennis and requested an Ambulance. Dennis was so emotionally destroyed he denied medical attention. The police took him to the emergency room anyway. Mainly to avoid any post arrest lawsuits.

Dennis was taken to the emergency room in handcuffs. He was immediately place on a gurney and given a bed. His left wrist was handcuffed to his bed with the Junior officer in his room. Dennis began to tell the cop his story and the cop just listened. Two hours past and Dennis received 13 stitches and two weeks of antibiotics. Dennis was again escorted to county jail.

Dennis was charged with criminal trespassing and assault and battery. Dennis began to cry as he was being booked in and fingerprinted.

I'm Leaving You For A White Woman

He was rapidly watching his life get flushed down the toilet. He was in the holding cell with one of his students. The student was Charles. Charles was one of his most unruly students. Charles began taunting Dennis and laughing, telling the other men in the cell "This fool is my English teacher." Dennis slumped on the bench, closed his eyes and pretended he was dreaming. But this wasn't a dream. It wasn't even a nightmare. Nightmare's end when you awake in fear, followed closely by a feeling of euphoric gratitude. This was hell in slow motion 3D. He felt La Ronda had a right to be upset but he also felt that the punishment didn't fit the crime.

La Ronda was known to overreact and over dramatize the slightest of situations. Her arrested developmental and perpetuate adolescent mindset justified the extreme reaction in cases where her feelings were involved.

Dennis was finally given a one-man cell. There he would remain until court. He was still to defeated to notify his family. His life had become a perpetual downward spiral. It all happened so fast. Once again, he found himself in jail for no apparent crime.

Dennis was angry. But his anger had no outlet to let off steam. If he were on the street, he'd have gone to the gym. But in jail, he could only turn his anger inward. It festered into a still lake of despair. He missed his first court-ordered visit behind bars. He was supposed to pick up Princess on the weekend he got arrested.

Dennis was debating whether or not to call Catherine collect. His visitation was already on shaky grounds. Dennis decided to call his sister Dana. Dana accepted his collect call. She was highly upset but not judgmental. Dana had agreed to come to court on Monday for support and to bail him out. Dana also agreed to call his job to request a substitute.

Monday morning came and Dennis was in court and Dana was there in the front row. The judge wasn't lenient at all. Dennis already had a domestic violence charge on his record. Undeserved as it may have been, it was still a violent conviction. Now here he is again just a year and a half after his domestic violence conviction. The judge set his bail amount at 50,000 dollars. His sister posted his bail. She knew that Dennis was good for it. Dennis was appreciative of his sister's consistent loyalty. Unfortunately, Dennis failed to tell Dana not to tell Florence

Dennis was released at 3pm that same day. As soon as Dana picked him up, Dennis expressed his gratitude. Dana immediately asked Dennis about her money. Dana didn't have the 10% of the 50,000 (which is 5,000) dollars so she emptied her bank account which was 1,700. She withdrew the remaining 3,300 from her and Derek's joint savings account.

Dana had withdrawn the money without notifying Derek. Dennis had to turn over his entire check to Dana. They had stopped at the bank on the way back from the cunty jail. He gave Dana 4,000 which left a balance of 1,000 stilled owed to her.

His 600-dollar child support was directly withdrawn from his checking account.

Dennis was left barely covering his rent. Dennis agreed to pay Dana back with his next paycheck. He felt obligated to tell her since she bailed him out. He saw the shocked look on her face. Dennis began to explain his visible cuts and scars on his face and arms. Dana told Dennis that La Ronda wasn't worth it. No woman was as Dana put it.

Dana told Dennis that Catherine was calling around looking for hm. Dana had also informed Dennis that she had told their mother where Dennis was. This infuriated Dennis because he knew his mother would tell her new best buddy Catherine. Dana took Dennis home after they left the bank, he went straight in and to a nice hot bath. He went to sleep immediately afterwards.

Tuesday morning when Dennis got to work, he noticed a memo in his box when he signed in. It was from Bill Toliver, the vice principal. Mr. Toliver requested to speak with Dennis immediately. The student Dennis ran into in the holding tank bailed out the same night. He apparently posted the encounter all over social media.

The story took on a life of its own. After a brief meeting, Dennis was told to clean out his desk at the end of the day. It was Bill who went to bat for Dennis and got him his job. Bill and Dennis had been apart of each other's lives since Dennis was a student and Bill was his English teacher.

Bill couldn't sweep these new charges under the rug. They were a bit too serious. Besides, the entire school, faculty and student body knew before Dennis arrived at work. Before the day ended, Bill visited Dennis's classroom. When the final bell rang, Bill stayed behind to help Dennis pack. Bill informed Dennis that his medical benefits would be good up to 90 days. After that, those too would be terminated. Bill wasn't talking to Dennis to belittle him. Nor was he enjoying being the barer of bad news.

He came by to do two things. 1) Throw him into deep waters. 2) To provide him with a boat. Bill Toliver's brother Bob owned and operated 'Big Bob's Landscaping'. Dennis was a proud college man who was a hair's throw away from his master's degree. Bill told Dennis to take the landscaping job for now. In one-year, Bill will have his record's sealed and he can go teach in a different school district.

Bill had already placed a call and convinced Bob to hire Dennis, it took some convincing, but he agreed to take the job. Bill handed Dennis Big Bob's information, then he escorted Dennis to the parking lot and off of school property. Dennis kept a stiff upper lip throughout the entire process, but he was hurt. He had disappointed his mentor, lost his job, but worst of all he had been removed from his passion, basketball. That's what hurt him the most.

Dennis drove home with three storage boxes filled with regret and memories. Normally, Dennis would call Tasha. He didn't want the incident to affect their friendship…but it already had. Dennis was losing interest in the counseling sessions. He enjoyed and appreciated having a place to vent and speak one on one to a sympathetic ear. As much as Dennis wanted to call La Ronda, he just couldn't bring himself to do it.

Florence called Dennis and began asking him how he's doing. Florence knew of his incarceration but not about his forced resignation. Dennis decided not to tell her about it. In fact, he decided not to tell her anything anymore about his personal life. Florence had a habit of gossiping and she was lonely. The two made for a toxic combination of indiscriminate lethal chatter.

During this conversation, Florence seemed to express genuine concern. Florence had gotten an earful from Catherine after Dennis didn't show up to pick Princess up from Catherine's house. Florence mentioned this to Dennis, and he was determined not to give her the satisfaction of a reaction. Instead, Dennis decided to just listen. Somewhere deep in the back of Florence's mind lurked the faint heart-felt vision of a Dennis and Catherine reconciliation. She was flighty optimistic about it.

When Catherine was alone with Florence, Catherine would tickle Florence's heart strings by toying with the idea. What are you going to do now? Dennis didn't know whether to tell her about the landscaping job. Since she was always telling Catherine what Dennis told her, he decided to gain sympathy from his own mother. Well, at least attempt to.

He informed his mother that he lost his job. She let out an aww. He could hear in her voice that she felt bad for him. Dennis didn't live with his mother, but his legal mailing address was his mom's house. His mom's address was also the address on his driver's license. The bad part about this was that Florence would receive his mail before him. Dennis was hoping Florence would tell Catherine about him losing his job. He thought maybe if Catherine knows he's not working, she'll excuse him for being short on his child support.

The job that Big Bob was offering paid only 500 per week in under the table tax-free cash. Just enough to keep him afloat. But not enough for swimming. This was a considerably lower amount of money that Dennis was accustomed to. And he was grateful to have it. Dennis ended his conversation early with his mother. He had a hard first day on the job in the morning.

Unsurprisingly, he couldn't sleep. He was a college man, and he'd never worked with his hands before. Bill all but guaranteed him another teaching job the next year in a neighboring district. That next year's job was what Dennis held his hopes on.

The next morning, Dennis was up and ready to go at 4:30am as instructed. He drove to the site dressed in jeans, flannel shirt and boots, resembling a lumber jack. Big Bob was expecting some well-dressed pansy. Dennis approached Bob ready to work. Dennis' first week was mostly training in an apprentice type situation. Dennis was still in night school and just weeks away from receiving his master's degree. Although he was 11 ½ months away from having the chance to use it. The work was hard on the body but easy on the mind. Dennis developed a new-found respect for The Blue Collar now that he'd worn both collars. Big Bob was as impressed as he was shocked. Dennis had a strong work ethic. Dennis also had a case pending that he was out on bail from. That impending reality would allow him only so much happiness. Dennis wisely refrained from telling anyone else besides his therapist about his new job and temporary career

Dennis missed his first appointment with his therapist since he began landscaping. His body was too worn down. It just wouldn't allow him to. He told himself he'd attend Friday's session no matter what. Catherine's new work schedule required she work on Friday nights. This gave Dennis more time to spend with Princess. Catherine would drop Princess off with Florence and Dennis would pick her up directly after his session. Anything that gave Dennis more time with Princess was great as far as he was concerned.

He was trying so hard to retain joint custody. That was when Dennis had his daughter every single weekend instead of every other weekend. Dennis walked into his session to tell his therapist that he was no longer teaching, and his insurance coverage would soon end. But never got the chance. His insurance company had already notified her of his current insurance status.

He had a little less than 3 months left. So, he decided to make the most of what was left. The therapist again informed Dennis about her group therapy sessions. Dennis wouldn't need insurance because her group sessions were free. The therapist volunteered her services at a local community center on the other side of the city.

She killed two birds with one stone. She loved her work of repairing the human spirit by repairing the human mind. Also, she used the group sessions as a tax write off. Because of that, everyone had to sign in, sign out and sign a receipt book. She wanted Dennis in her group sessions so he could benefit from similar stories.

Dennis began his session with a recap of his most recent events. He felt his present was more important than his past given the circumstances. He began with Daphne's party. He went over the event in detail. The more he spoke, the more disdain he began to feel for the opposite sex. These feeling didn't manifest towards the therapist.

Dennis spoke about La Ronda and what he loved about her, what he missed about her. He told his therapist about how he was issued a restraining order when he bailed out of jail. The case wasn't over. He was facing very serious charges. His next court date was two months from now.

The therapist reaffirmed that their sessions were under the doctor-client privilege. And she couldn't be called to testify for or against him. That was a load off his shoulders. He was scared he would be depicted as crazy. It was bad enough La Ronda and her parents had a restraining order against him.

I'm Leaving You For A White Woman

The fact that Dana's man Derek brought Byron to the party added the right amount of insult to his injury. By the time the session ended, Dennis was yet again exhausted. He had a slight headache. He drove straight to his mom's house to pick up Princess.

When he walked in, he was so glad Catherine wasn't there. Princess saw her father and ran towards him jumping into his arms. She was so happy, she cried tears of joy. His mother took a picture of the two of them standing by the door. Then they left.

Dennis had not yet been home that day and Princess was hungry. So, he decided to take her to a pizza parlor that had video games. Dennis and Princess were having the time of their lives. They were playing air hockey and Dennis was letting Princess win. A white woman approached the two of them and asked could she and her nephew play next game. Dennis told the white woman that he and his daughter planned to play all night. But he was willing to compromise. Dennis proposed that since it was only one air hockey table they could alternate. The woman agreed.

While Dennis was speaking to the woman, Princess seized the moment and scored the winning goal. Dennis began to laugh and the two of them released the table to the woman and her nephew. After a few minutes, their order was ready. "Alexander, Party of two!" They enjoyed a large peperoni and black olive pizza. Princess began to tell her father about what's new on her school's playground.

Dennis was in heaven whenever he was with his Princess. She was definitely a Daddy's girl. Princess began to talk about some boy in her classroom that keeps kicking the back of her chair. She said sometimes he pulls her ponytails when the teacher isn't looking. Dennis told princess that the boy probably likes her. Princess let out a big "Yuck!" They both started to laugh and continued eating. Both were just enjoying the night

The woman had signaled to Dennis to come and get on the air hockey table. She was holding it for them. When Princess and Dennis briskly walked over to the air hockey table, the woman and her nephew came and sat at Dennis's booth. That way they could sit and wait on their order as well as watch Dennis and Princess pizza. As Princess and her father began to play their game, the woman's order was called "Simmons, Party of two, your order is ready!"

The woman's nephew got up to get the order while Ms. Simmons waited at the Alexander table. The nephew came back to the table with their order. Dennis and Princess finished their game 5 minutes later and waved to Ms. Simmons. Ms. Simmons and nephew gestured in a way to let them know that they were finished with Air hockey. They were too involved in eating their pizza.

Dennis and Princess came back to the table to finish their meal. Ms. Simmons and her nephew were still at the table. "I hope you guys don't mind, there were no empty tables and I." Dennis cut her off by saying "It's quite all right." The four of them ate til getting so full that all of them were a little sleepy. Besides, it was past 9pm and Dennis had a long day.

Dennis and Ms. Simmons began light small talk. Witty banter and puns back and forth flying over the children's heads. As it hit 9:21pm, all four of them mutually agreed that it was time to leave. Especially since the kids were both yawning. Out in the parking lot, they both said their goodbyes and went in opposite directions to where their cars were parked.

"Did you have a good time?" Dennis asked Princess.

"Yep! Sorry I beat you so bad in air hockey daddy."

They both laughed as Dennis threw his car in reverse. The car went backwards close to 3 feet before Dennis put his right arm behind the passenger's seat to look out of the back window. Right when he looked back, he hit the driver's side rear door of Ms. Simmons car. "Smash!" Then Dennis pulled forward back in the parking space. He got out to inspect the damage. "You must not want me to go" said Ms. Simmons whose car he'd just hit.

First, they both were taken back, surprised by the coincidence. They exchanged telephone numbers, insurance and driver's license information. Both cars were still drivable so they both drove off instead of blocking the exit and

causing a scene. Most of the damage was on Ms.
Simmons car. Dennis lost a taillight in the accident.
Princess fell asleep on the way home. As
long as his daughter was happy, then so was he.
When he got home, he didn't wake up Princess.
Dennis carried her upstairs and place her in the bed.
Even with today's events, Dennis went to bed
happy.

The next morning, Dennis and Princess
picked up Florence. On Saturday morning Florence
usually cooked breakfast for herself and Dennis. It
was an Alexander tradition no matter what they
were going through. Today she didn't have to cook.
The three of them went to a nice old fashioned
American styled diner.

Dennis was enjoying his day out with his
family. His cell phone rang, and he put it on silent.
Since things were going so well, he didn't want any
kind of interference. He figured he'd check his
messages and return the call later. While they were
eating, Florence asked Princess how her mother
Catherine was doing. Dennis just smiled and
pretended to show interest. Catherine was still
Princess' mother. Dennis made it a point not to
speak ill of Catherine when Princess was present. If
he couldn't say something positive, he wouldn't say
anything at all. Princess replied to her grandmother
in traditional kid fashion "Mommy's fine grandma."
Then Florence kept digging.

"Did she have class this weekend?"

"No, she went out of town with her boyfriend grandma."

Dennis didn't bite on that comment. He actually surprised himself by the fact that he didn't care. It went through one ear and out the other. He was proud of himself. That was when he realized that he was completely over Catherine. For the first time in a long time, Dennis felt confident. His confidence came from a new-found love for himself. The therapy, his experiences, were all working on him from the inside. In time he felt sure that he would get his joint custody back. But for now, he was content with what he had.

Florence was disappointed to hear about Catherine's boyfriend. She was slightly hurt that "Cathy" was dating. More so, she was insulted that Catherine didn't tell her gossip buddy Florence. After breakfast, Florence still wanted to hang out with her son and granddaughter. Dennis wasn't in the mood to spend all day with anyone but Princess. As they were finishing breakfast, Florence asked about Dennis's job. Dennis almost spoke about it but held his tongue at the last minute. He told his mother that he was still looking. Dennis hated lying to his mother, but he knew she was basically a spy for Catherine.

After breakfast, Dennis took his mom home. Then he and Princess went back to his house. Dennis wanted Princess to get comfortable being over at his house again. She had friends on his street. His daughter ran straight to her room and got her skates.

"Daddy can I go outside?"

"Can you?"

"I mean, may I?"

"Yes, you may" answered Dennis.

He was still a teacher at heart. Dennis, the overprotective father went outside to watch his daughter skate up and down the street with a few of the neighborhood kids. Dennis took this time to turn his ringer back on. When he checked his messages, a woman left a message about the car accident. It was Ms. Simmons, the woman he met by accident at the pizza parlor.
Her name was Jackie Simmons." Hello, it's me the woman from last night, Jackie. Um I decided not to evolve you in the accident report. I told the insurance company it was a hit and run. But I do need the 250-dollar deductible. Okay, give me a call. Ciao!" There was also a message from Tasha. She left a message saying she heard he lost his job, so she offered him a loan of an undisclosed amount if he needed it.

Dennis missed talking to Tasha. He was planning to call Jackie back first. Dennis always returned calls in the order in which they called. So he called Jackie back first. She was delighted that he called back so quickly. Dennis agreed to pay the 250-dudctible. They both set the exchange for the pizza parlor where they first met.

6pm was the time they set. As it started getting late, Dennis called his daughter in. Dennis told his daughter to take a bath. Princess thought that meant to go to bed. Dennis said she didn't have to go to bed but to put on her pajamas because they were in for the night. While Princess was in the tub, Dennis began cooking dinner for the two of them.

Dennis made sure Princess didn't eat too much junk food. He did his best to keep the fast food to a minimum. Catherine called to speak to Princess. As much as Dennis didn't want Catherine calling during his time, he allowed it. Princess was out of the bathtub and in her pajamas at the table.

Dennis rarely had vegetables in his refrigerator. He was a stereotypical bachelor. No matter how many times Princess came over or didn't come over, Dennis always kept her a bedroom of her own. He read her a story and tucked her in. Dennis called Tasha back after Princess fell asleep and Tasha was happy and surprised Dennis had called her back. Especially since it was during a Princess weekend.

Dennis wouldn't take Tasha's offer but appreciated the gesture. He told Tasha he had some money saved up. He still didn't want anyone to know what he was doing. Dennis was grateful for the landscaping job. But also slightly ashamed.

When they woke up Sunday, the two of them got dressed for church. Princess loved going to church with her father. Dennis only went to church with Princess. On the weekends that she wasn't with him, he didn't go. Dennis wasn't particularly a religious man, but he wanted his daughter to have a good spiritual relationship with God.

After church, Dennis had to drop Princess and his mother off. 5 o'clock pm was the designated pick up time. Catherine would only pick up and drop off Princess at Florence's house. It was even stated in the court ordered visitation paperwork.

Dennis drove home quickly. He didn't want to run into Catherine on the street. A small part of him still resented Catherine for dragging him into court for more money and less visitation. Besides, Dennis had to be at work early Monday morning. So as long as Dennis was in the landscaping business, he knew he couldn't have any late Sunday nights.

The next morning, he went to work as usual. He had agreed to attend the therapist group session Saturday at the community center. Dennis still had a few private sessions left that his lapsed insurance still covered. Dennis figured he might as well continue until the coverage ran out.

Chapter 8

He was starting to get use to his new job.
No longer did his body feel so sore after work. This
time when he got off work, he drove straight to the
pizza parlor. He walked in a little before 6pm and
sat in a booth. He ordered a small pepperoni pizza
and a diet soda while he waited.

At 6:05pm Jackie Simmons walks in and
slid into Dennis' booth. She helped herself to a slice
of pizza without being offered and began to speak.
The pizza cheese was still hot. Jackie attempted to
talk but the pizza had begun to burn the roof of her
mouth. Jackie then snatched Dennis diet soda right

out of his hand and guzzled half of it. Dennis was overtaken by her level of comfort.

"I see you're a man of your word. Punctual too, your wife must be bored to death" Jackie said and began to chuckle.

"I'm not married." Answered Dennis

"Oh, smart too."

"The only woman in my life is my daughter."

"Why'd your wife leave? What was it? Infidelity? Erectile disfunction?"

"No, my daughter's mom was sexually satisfied."

"Really? What's your secret?"

"Jackie, if I told you I'd have to kill you. It's that top secret."

Jackie began to giggle. She poked out her bottom lip as to pout and asked,

"Please tell me?" she replied in her mocking baby voice.

"I can't, its illegal in 37 states."

They both began to laugh. The waitress came over to the table and asked if they would like another order or a refill. Dennis asked for a refill of his diet soda. The waitress asked, "How long have you two been together?" Both Jackie and Dennis were tongue tied. Then the waitress continued "I didn't mean to put you guys on the spot. It's just rare that I see a couple with so much chemistry. How did you meet?" "By accident" said Jackie. Both Jackie and Dennis began to laugh hysterically.

Jackie Simmons seemed to be a nice, bubbly, take life by the horn's white girl. Dennis had enjoyed the banter and company that evening. Jackie got up to leave and looked back at Dennis and asked, "Will you walk me to my car?" "sure" Dennis replied. Dennis left a tip on the table. Then Jackie paid for the pizza at the counter. Dennis tried to stop her, but Jackie insisted and said "It's the least I can do. I mean you just gave me 250 bucks."

As Dennis held the door open to let Jackie exit first, she stopped I the doorway looked him in the eyes and said, "You'll get the next one." Just before she got into her still dented car, she looked Dennis in the eyes again and said, "Well you have my number." Then she drove away waving.

Dennis paid her very little mind. He was still exhausted from work. Jackie was flirting as hard as she could. But Dennis didn't have his mind on women of any race. He was still on a natural high from an extraordinary visit with his daughter. Dennis didn't see Catherine's unprovoked legal fight coming. She was so close to his mother he wouldn't have thought it in a million years.

The days went by at a normal pace. His life and activities were slowing to a pace where he could stop the perpetual downward spiral and begin its ascend back to where it once was. His child support had stopped being deducted from his check since he no longer taught at the high school. But that didn't stop Dennis from paying the ordered amount. Dennis would leave 600 dollars at his mother's house and the next day after work he'd pick up a signed and dated receipt. He had purchased a receipt book form a stationary store, strictly for records of his cash payments.

He never thought Catherine would stoop so low. At this point he figured there's nothing she wouldn't do to hurt him in some way or another. Dennis was saving as much money as he could in his top drawer. All cash since he was avoiding banks. Dennis was showing signs of a new attitude. There was a little more pep in his step.

When Dennis was teaching, he was in a different state of mind. He still owed money on his BMW which had 3 years of payments left. Dennis did the unthinkable, the unbelievable. He stopped paying his car note two months back so the bank could do a voluntary repossession. Then he paid cash in full for a small compact Japanese car.

It appeared as if he were downsizing but Dennis didn't see it that way. He saw it as maturing. Passing a milestone in his life. Besides, since the increase in child support this seemed to be the smart decision. Only now the compact car was missing a rear driver's side taillight, due to the accident.

Dennis had called Tasha to get some insight on a hunch he had. He explained to her in detail about the accident. Dennis told Tasha everything about Jackie except her race. Tasha felt Jackie was definitely flirting and expected Dennis to call her. Tasha was the only one Dennis felt he could tell almost everything. He didn't trust any other woman beside her and his therapist. He and Tasha were almost back to where they were as friends before Daphne's party. But he still didn't tell Tasha where he worked. He decided that Tasha may slip up and tell Daphne at work. Daphne would for sure tell everyone she knew

He was in the process of eliminating negativity out of his life. Dennis needed that conversation with Tasha. He also thought Jackie was giving him signals, but as a man he figured he may have been delusional. Dennis came up with excuse after excuse why not to call Jackie. But the truth was that Dennis was scared. He wasn't completely over La Ronda. Dennis also harbored resentment toward Catherine. He blamed Catherine for coming into his family and distancing Florence from Dennis and Dana.

He personally felt he was in no emotional state to date someone new at this time. At the risk of hurting Jackie's feelings by ignoring her advances, Dennis decided to call her and let her down easy. He figured at best they could possibly develop a friendship. This was how he met Tasha. His aunt Daphne befriended Tasha ant work. They began carpooling with one another. Shortly thereafter Daphne introduced Tasha to Dennis.

Dennis and Tasha weren't compatible on a romantic level. But they both discovered that they were both great unjudgmental listeners. He found a confidant from an unsuccessful hook up. Aside from one night while they both were single. Tasha and Dennis' relationship had remained strictly platonic. Based on that alone, Dennis decided he'd call Jackie.

In an instant, he located her number in his cell phone's caller ID and called her. As the phone started to ring, Dennis began to get nervous. What do I say? What if she was just being nice? What if? What if? What if? Dennis was so relieved when the phone's voice mail came on. He became anxious as he waited to hear the beep. BEEP! "Hi, um hello, this is Dennis Alexander. I'm calling to see if you're doing okay and if you'd like to hang out sometime. Um.... Well, give me a call, let me know." Then Dennis hung up.

That wasn't so hard, he thought. Within 10 minutes Jackie returned his call.

"Hey, you called me what's up?"

"Did you get my message?"

"No, I haven't checked my messages yet. I saw your number on my caller ID."

"Yea I was just calling to see if you'd like to go out sometime. You know, to maybe grab bite."

"I see no reason why we can't. But hey! Let me drive."

"Ha, ha" Dennis sarcastically mockingly replied.

"How about I pick you up Friday night?"
"Okay but I'm still driving "Jackie replied.

Dennis then told her he'd call her back later if she wanted to talk. Jackie said she'd call him after she left the gym. When they hung up the phone, Dennis was relieved that he wasn't delusional and there was a connection between them.
Dennis had never considered dating outside his race. He was nervous about it not working and scared it would work. His first though was how would his family react. Then a feeling of not caring how they felt occupied the majority of his thoughts.
Dennis called Catherine to speak to Princess. Catherine gave Princess the phone without speaking to him. He actually preferred it that way. He spoke to Princess for 15 minutes. He was flattered. He knew that 15 minutes was like 2 hours in adult time. Princess loved speaking on the phone period. But especially to her father.
Later that night, Dennis called Jackie and she answered the phone on the first ring. Dennis began the conversation by asking her about her activities at the gym. Jackie was athletic. She played softball in college. Now she worked as a massage therapist for a chiropractor. Most of her clients were in car accidents. They would get their backs adjusted then go right next door for massage therapy.
Dennis had told her about his college basketball days. Jackie took the time right there to invite Dennis to her family picnic. Dennis implied

that they weren't ready for family introductions yet. But Jackie told Dennis that at the family picnic they played basketball, and Jackie wanted him on her team.

"Isn't that cheating?" asked Dennis.

"Hey, the last two games we got our butts kicked. And yes, it is cheating" Jackie laughingly replied.

Dennis agreed to play. Mainly because he missed coaching the high school team. Basketball was still his passion. He couldn't go a week without watching a game during basketball season. They talked all night. Dennis let time escape him. He knew he had to be up early for work.

Big Bob got started early. Dennis was determined not to ever be late or absent at work. He wanted Bill Toliver to know how appreciative he was for the job. Without the landscaping job, Dennis might have ended up homeless. He treated the landscaping job like the lifesaver it was. Truth is, he only took the 11th grade English job because it came with the basketball coaching job.

Days had past and with each passing night, Dennis and Jackie spoke all every night. After the first two days, he and Jackie toned it down so it wouldn't keep him from waking up early. They would only talk til 9pm.

Dennis asked Jackie what attracted her to him? She said she liked the way he interacted with his daughter. That was a big turn-on to Jackie. She figured if he could bring that much happiness to a child then how much happiness could he bring to a woman. Jackie asked Dennis what attracted him to her? Dennis said her witty banter with the waitress. He felt she had the right spirit for him. Neither one of them mentioned race. Neither of them though it mattered. Jackie had broken up with her boyfriend two years ago. She said she'd been enjoying her single life ever since. She'd recently been on several first dates but only a few second ones and no third ones.

Dennis didn't tell Jackie about his sessions with a relationship counselor/therapist. Plus, he liked where he was mentally and spiritually. Dennis' therapy was beginning to go into a slightly different direction. He had grown fond of his therapy sessions. His therapist had him pull up the wrinkles of his past so she could iron them out in the present.

Dennis wanted to discuss what happened at the party with Jasmine. That was the event which lead to the negative events in La Ronda livingroom, which caused him to lose his job. His therapist told him that the present was irrelevant if the past wasn't ironed out. Once the past was ironed out, it would immediately fix the problems in the present without Dennis even knowing. There were still a couple of issues, demons if you will, that Dennis was yet to confront.

When Dennis got to his session, the therapist had bad news for him. She had miscalculated the length of time left on his insurance. She though his coverage would run out in 2 to 3 months. Turns out it runs out in 2 to 3 weeks. As in 1 to 2 more sessions.

Therefore, it was time to turn up the heat. She couldn't depend on Dennis to show up on a Saturday to her volunteer group therapy sessions. She offered Dennis 15 extra minutes for the last few sessions, just in case Dennis wasn't going to show up Saturday she could close his file. A closed file represented a solved problem.

She was the best in the business. Dennis had his mind fixated on attending at least 2 months' worth of sessions. The therapist wanted to go further back.

"Tell me about your father." This threw him for a loop.

"He's dead" Dennis answering as if that were all he planned to say.

"But your parents were divorced when he passed away, correct?"

"Yea" answered Dennis in a defensive tone.

"Dennis, my questions may hurt, the same as it may hurt to extract a rotten tooth. But trust me, the pain of ignoring the tooth will hurt much worse and cause much more damage down the road. Let me do what I can to clear the runway for your present and future tooth or relationships if you will."

I'm Leaving You For A White Woman

Dennis held up both hands indicating for her to continue.

"Tell me about your father" the therapist once again asked the same question in the same tone.

"He was my hero. He died of a heart attack."

Dennis kept starting the story at the time of his death. He went on to talk about how his father would take him and his sister to NBA Basketball games. How his father was a man of few words. He never heard his parents argue until the night his father moved out. After their divorce, Dennis didn't see his father much.

He died a few years later. The therapist was arranging her notes and writing as fast as Dennis was talking. She always gave her patients an assessment of their sessions. It served as a prescription of sorts. She had just one more private session left with him. Dennis' critique of his father soon shifted to his mother. He loved both of his parents. But his daughter was his heart and soul.

Dennis had no story to tell. He was so anxious to get his assessment for next week. He considered them answers to a test. A test called his life. Dennis talked as the therapist just wrote. He babbled mostly but stayed away from the subject of his father. He spoke more about his mother. He compared how she was before his father left and after his father left. Then how she reacted to his death.

He saw his mother go through three different stages of development. Dennis didn't have any more stories to tell the therapist. None that she needed to hear he felt.

She looked Dennis in the eyes and told him that he was dating someone new. Dennis was surprised because he hadn't told anyone about Jackie. He was too afraid of something going wrong. He felt that he was ready to live again. He knew by the way he felt that he'd be over La Ronda soon.

He was insulted by the restraining order. It made him feel as if La Ronda regarded him as a stalker. La Ronda knew Dennis didn't come to her house to hurt anyone. When she took Byron's side against his, it hurt deep in his soul. Since the incident, Dennis hadn't been able to speak to Dana's boyfriend Derek or look him in the face. Dennis knew that Derek had nothing to do with Byron and La Ronda. But still, if La Ronda was able to be taken away so easily then she wasn't the one. Deep down he himself knew that.

That was the logic he slept with every night. Truth is, he was more embarrassed than anything else. That scene was the last thing Dennis wanted Catherine to see. He knew some day in some way Catherine would use it against him. He also knew that Catherine would tell his mother, and his mother would tell him.

Dennis was bracing himself for the emotional punch in the gut. Princess was his heart and Catherine had sole custody of Princess. This meant Catherine had his heart in her hands. This one fact kept Dennis in a never-ending state of worry. He knew Catherine was vindictive and bitter. But Catherine had a boyfriend, according to

Princess. Whenever Catherine was involved with a man, she virtually ignored Dennis. But as soon as something in her relationship went wrong, she'd turn her attention to Dennis. Consciously or subconsciously Catherine took out her frustration and hatred of all men on Dennis. Even the deep-rooted hatred and disdain she had for her father who abandoned her and the uncle who molested her as a child.

Dennis was asked about his sister Dana. This question didn't invoke his silence. He actually adjusted his position on the couch and a sly smile horizontally appeared. Dennis loved Dana. He saw her as his protector. It was Dana who helped him as a teenager through his socially awkward period in Jr high school. To Dennis, Dana could do no wrong. She was his hero after the death of their father.

They had developed a friendship as siblings. Dana took it personally when Dennis was taken advantage of by women. Dana hated Catherine although she was always respectful and cordial in her presence. Catherine didn't like Dana either. Florence would put Catherine against Dana and refer to them both as her "daughters."

Dana was also jealous of Florence and Catherine's relationship. Florence would jump through hoops for Princess but not for Dana's 3 yr. old son Jason. Whenever Catherine needed a babysitter, she'd dump Princess off with Florence without calling.

Florence never turned her away. But when it came to Dana it was another story. Dana had to make an appointment in advance. Florence would reluctantly agree to babysit only after a lot of begging and never for free. Daphne also acted as an ally of Catherine's to show her allegiance to her sister Florence. Florence knowingly did this to help sew up the wound left from empty nest syndrome. Most of the Alexander's wanted nothing to do with Catherine. Florence aligned herself with Catherine so she could act as a co-parent with Catherine. Catherine used Florence to hurt Dennis. Dennis felt betrayed on so many levels. The only thing that kept him sane was Princess.

He was accustomed to full-time fatherhood. Seeing his daughter every other weekend was next to impossible to get use to. After the session, Dennis wasn't exhausted. In fact, he felt energized, not exhausted like usual.

As soon as he left, he called Jackie. She was just getting to her car. Jackie had begun to tell Dennis about the day. The two had agreed to go walking along the beach. Dennis planned to pick her up later that night for dinner. Florence had called him to tell her that she was ill. She told him that Dana was going to take her to the hospital. She said she'd call him from her hospital room when she knew anything.

Dennis said okay but Florence was heavy on his mind. She was a diabetic who ignored her diet. Dennis went home and took a long shower. Working around so many different types of grass made him itchy. Dennis took a long shower every day when he got home from work. Then another when he went to bed.

I'm Leaving You For A White Woman

His body was adjusting fine to the manual labor he was putting it through. Somehow, some way, Dennis was rebuilding his self-esteem through therapy and working with his hands. Landscaping had acted as an outlet for his creativity and aggression. He would lose time in his work. Since it required a lot of alone time, there wasn't anyone there to speak to. It forced Dennis to be with Dennis. Being alone with his thoughts, isolating himself from distractions provided him, with moments of clarity.

Even though Dennis wished to return to teaching he was no longer letting the lack thereof depress him. He was not letting his work define him anymore. Unbeknown to Dennis, he'd achieved a major breakthrough in therapy.

Dennis went to pick up Jackie. She greeted him with a kiss at the door. It was their first kiss. It came without warning. Dennis kissed her back as the kiss went from a peck to French. Dennis walked Jackie back into her apartment as the two undressed each other while lips were locked. Neither of the two allowing their lips to separate. He and Jackie never made it to the bedroom. They didn't even get as far as the couch. They did manage to close the front door. They made love as if they had met in another life. This was the first interracial sexual experience for both of them. Though it didn't seem to matter to either of them enough to comment on nor point out.

When they finished, there was 15 minutes of afterglow. Then they both showered together which led to heavy petting in the shower. Third base if you will. Jackie looked into Dennis's eyes and felt his pain. As tears ran down his face Jackie began to cry also. Jackie had also been though an emotionally sterile relationship.

Dennis and his unprotected heart needed to be handled with appreciative care. Jackie could feel his vulnerability. All she ever wanted was a man who wouldn't hurt her. As that thought crossed her mind, he leaned back and said, "Please don't hurt me." Jackie began kissing and licking his tears.

Jackie always wanted was a man who didn't need to wear his machismo on his shoulder. She was visually stunning with a swimmer's build. She wanted a man in her life who didn't feel the need to impress her. But could be open an honest with her. In the shower they just held each other then began to bathe one another.

The two hearts met and melted into each other. Words were no longer necessary. Dennis held Jackie from behind in a hug as they rocked from side to side slowly to the music playing on her bathroom radio. They got dressed without saying a word then headed to the restaurant.

At the restaurant, Jackie began telling Dennis about their agenda tomorrow and what tomorrow meant to her family. Jackie's father organized a basketball game with his family against the family of a co-worker. That was over ten years ago. They'd meet and play against each other twice a year. The Simmons family had lost the last 4 in a row by 6 points or more.

After hearing that, Dennis knew he was going to attend and participate. Especially since there's a 'no hard feelings' feast afterwards. Dennis had gotten really hungry. Right when the food came Dennis received a text form Dana. 'Momma is okay. We're all at the hospital in room 2804.' Just then they got the food to go.

"What's up? What's going on honey."

"My mom is in the hospital."

"Oh, is it serious?"

"My sister says she's okay" Dennis replied.

The waitress boxed up the food and they left. They arrived at the hospital and went straight to the room. Dana, Derek and Catherine were standing around Florence who was in bed. The entire room went silent when Dennis and Jackie walked in. Dennis began to ask his mother how she was doing.

"What did the doctor say momma?" Florence looked at Jackie. Then she made eye contact with everyone in the room before answering.

"Oh…um..oh the Doc said I can go home tomorrow. I got carried away. Red Velvet Cake and some Bar-B-Q. My sugar was 510" explained Florence.

Dennis was upset. He'd warned his mother over and over about taking her diabetes more

seriously. At that moment Dennis realized Jackie
was with him unintroduced.

"Momma, everybody this is Jackie. Jackie that's my
daughter's mom Catherine. That's my sister Dana
and her boyfriend Derek."

"Hello" said Derek as he smiled and shook her
hand.

"And this is my mom Florence."

"How do you do?" said Florence.

All eyes were on Jackie.
"So, you're a friend of Dennis?" Dana asked.
Because no one else was going to. Dana directed
her question at Jackie. Jackie smiled and looked at
Dennis as he said, "She's my girlfriend." Jackie
looked back at Dana smiled, raised an eyebrow,
then hugged Dennis's left arm all in one motion.
Derek looked right at Dennis, nodded his head and
smiled.

Dennis kissed his mother on the forehead
and he and Jackie left. He didn't throw Jackie in
their faces nor did he hide her or his feelings.
Jackie was surprised and proud that Dennis claimed
her as his girlfriend. She was a blonde but not
stupid. To her this meant she wasn't a one-night
stand. And that was her biggest fear.

As soon as they got in the car, Jackie
grabbed Dennis's face with both her hands and
frenched kissed Dennis for minutes.

I'm Leaving You For A White Woman

"Wow, what was that about?" asked Dennis.

"For being you. Just for being you" answered Jackie. Then she continued as they left the parking lot.

"Can we go to your place?"

"We can go anywhere you wish" answered Dennis.

They drove straight to his house. He was renting a house he could easily afford when he was teaching but as a landscaper he held on oft times by a thread. When they walked in, the first thing Jackie noticed was a big degree on the wall that read "Dennis Alexander." Her eyes panned to the right of it and the other one that read "Masters."

Jackie was notably impressed with his degree's, but she was more impressed with his many baseball trophies on display. "Wow, I know you told me you played basketball. But I didn't know you played! played! Wow" said Jackie.

Jackie began to set the table by going through Dennis' kitchen. Dennis put the 'to-go' food in the microwave to warm it up. Then he and Jackie went to go wash their hands. They sat and had dinner, then relaxed on the couch and watched movies like an old married couple.

Saturday's game stared at 1pm. Dennis planned to attend the Saturday group session in the morning. Jackie was planning to spend the night with Dennis. He set his alarm for 7am because the group was from 8am to 9am. He told Jackie he had a meeting to attend. Jackie leaned into him and replied "Okay babe. I'll be here when you get back."

Dennis began to explain the reason why and what's it for. He wanted to be 100% honest with Jackie. He felt it was very important that she trusted him. When he began to explain where and why Jackie cut him off and said "I trust you babe. You don't owe me an explanation."
Dennis wasn't familiar with being treated like an adult or treated like a man by a woman. He'd grown comfortable to typical black women responses based in insecurity and subconscious hatred for black men stimming from their non-existent relationships with their fathers. Dennis was at ease, finally. Her comment alone drove his testosterone levels up 300% so they made love again but this time they took their time. Candles, music and satin pajamas.

"Are we moving too fast?" she asked.

"My heart is dictating my pace" answered Dennis.

Jackie smiled and agreed. The next morning Dennis woke Jackie up with breakfast in bed.

"Wow, no man has ever spoiled me like this before. Be careful babe, a girl could get use to this."

"I sure hope so" Dennis replied as he walked out the door.

Chapter 9

Dennis walked in and the group was already in progress even though he was 10 minutes early. Dennis looked around and didn't recognize any of the gentlemen. But he recognized the mood. Tired black men, all 6 of them. The therapist's face expressed gratitude at the sight of Dennis in the doorway. He wanted to please his therapist. He felt that she had done so much for him.

Dennis wanted to do something for her. His participation was his way of saying thank you. He has wanted to give her some kind of gift within the boundaries of doctor patient relationship.

Dennis instantly felt the energy of the group. Even if he never came back, he was glad he had decided to attend. "Dennis, delighted you could come. Everyone this is Dennis." The men in the circle of chairs leaned back and welcomed Dennis "Hello Dennis!" The group replied in unison.

As the therapist made space for Dennis, she introduced the members of the group individually. "Derrick" "Edward" "Robert" "Jeffery" "Gregory"

"Carl." "Edward continue" the therapist said. Edward resumed speaking where he had left off. Dennis figured he'd jump in whenever relevant. Edward wanted to save his relationship with his longtime girlfriend Mary.

Edward's gripe was that when he was the breadwinner in the relationship, Mary would cook for him. They shared the cleaning, but Mary did most of the cooking. When Edward's finances changed, so did Mary's behavior and treatment of him.

She would make comments and sly remarks about his inadequacies in private and public. "How would this make you feel?" asked the therapist. Edward said it made him angry. Sometimes violently angry. He never hit her, but he damaged property. It made him feel stupid because all of the time, energy, effort and money he spent. He said it was like she put a monetary value on their relationship.

"Jeffery, do you have anything to share?"

"Not really. My old lady and I have been smooth sailing. I take your lessons home and she and do them. Those mutual respect exercises."

"Okay, who has something to share?" Jeffery cut her off before she could ask another question.

"I do have something to add."

"Okay, you have the floor."

I'm Leaving You For A White Woman

Jeffery spent a lot of evenings with his newlywed wife, Tomika. It was rocky at the beginning, but they'd seemed to have worked it out. They'd watch games shows together on the couch in the evenings. Instead of excluding Tomika, he began including her and the entire relationship changed for the better.

Jeffery's gripe was the media and the overt disrespect of black men. America's society at large and it's disdain for black men. He pointed out that talk shows with black female host seemed to introduce white male guest (actors) and handsome, adorable or gorgeous. How they seem to cater to them. But they don't refer to black male (actors) in the same way.

Jeffery went on to say how a lot of black women bought into the stereotype or myth of the 'black brute.' How does a single black mother who hates black men, raise a black son to love himself as a soon to be black man? As Dennis looked around, he saw the other men nodding their heads in agreement.

Dennis didn't wish to participate in the discussion, but he was listening. He was taking in what he could. But Dennis wasn't as unhappy as he once was. He wasn't surprised to hear some of the complaints from the other men. But now he was beginning to see the therapist's interest in his contribution to the group. His opinion and story were only a microcosm of a broad-based problem.

Dennis had been searching for a solution to the problems within himself. The reason he couldn't find the root of the problem is because he was looking in the wrong place. Dennis didn't want to be rude, but he only had time for one more share.

"Does anyone else have anything to hare?"

"I do" Robert answered.

Robert was "Whipped" to say the least. Out of all of the stories Dennis listened to, Robert's struck a nerve. Robert was in an abusive relationship with a black woman he pursued since high school. What made Robert's story so unique was the fact that Robert was the abused victim who blamed himself.

He caught it from a multitude of angles. Robert had left his family in West Virginia to be with Stacy. Once Robert was far away from his family support and friends, Stacy began to change. She had become a bully.

Anytime Robert stood up, she'd make sure he had no legs to stand on. She treated him like she owned him. She would sabotage any efforts he made to progress. One-night, Robert came home late from working overtime and Stacy beat him with a baseball bat. She had accused him of an affair. When the police showed up, Stacy accused him of beating her. With no visible injuries to Stacy the police still arrested Robert. He was taken to the emergence room. He suffered a skull facture and a broken rib. Stacy was not arrested.

Robert ended up with Domestic Violence classes after 120 days in jail. The classes lasted a year (52 weeks). Since Robert had nowhere to live when he left jail, he went back to Stacy. Stacy was a small woman in stature but would react violently to any comment that she deemed disrespectful. Her first response was always physical violence with a verbal assault as a precursor. She spoke in a language Robert referred to as 'Yellingese.' She took deep breaths and shouted commands while exhaling with the tone of a drill sergeant.

As pretty as she was, Stacy lacked femininity. She cursed like a man. Robert felt like a failure whenever he told Stacy he was leaving her or moving out. Stacy would cry and beg him to stay. Robert felt he was abandoning Stacy and her son whenever he got fed up enough to leave her.

Stacy loved Robert in her own sick twisted way. She learned how to love this way from an abusive mother in her childhood. She felt it was normal to whip her son with a belt whenever he made a mistake. Hearing Robert explain how this was all his fault and he deserved to be treated this way stuck to Dennis.

Dennis didn't want to leave. Especially since he didn't get a chance to share, but he had to. Dennis stood u to properly excuse himself. He was glad he had gone but felt a little uneasy in the group. He had gotten use to the one on one relationship between patient and psychologist.

Dennis got back home and found Jackie dressed and ready to go. They left to go to Jackie's house to picked up some equipment. They had basketballs, towels and sports bottles. Jackie and Dennis loaded everything into Jackie's car.

Since she knew where they were going it just made sense for her to drive. When they arrived at the park, Dennis grabbed the gear and Jackie grabbed him by the arm. They put the gear on the picnic table. Both families were pulling up in spirts.

The other family, The Rignelli Family were putting on their red and white shirts. The Simmons family were in their traditional green and white shirts. Jackie had walked right up to her father and introduced Dennis as her new boyfriend. Her father introduced himself as Phillip and asked Dennis one question

"Can you play?"

"I'm pretty good sir."

"Suit up!"

As soon as the Rignelli's hit the court, Mike Rignelli said;

"Woe, woe, who's this guy?" referring to Dennis. Phillip replied quickly,

"He's my daughter's boyfriend."

"That's bull. What's the matter, scared of another whipping, huh? You went out and hired a ringer?"

"You said girlfriends, boyfriends and in-laws were fair game did you not?" Phillip asked.

"He has to prove it. Jackie give your so-called boyfriend a kiss" Mike demanded.

Dennis was nervous. There he was, in the middle of the basketball court frozen stiff. He had a goofy grin on his face. Jackie walked briskly over to Dennis and gave him a 10 second French kiss. Then Jackie turned to her father Phillip. Phillip shrugged his shoulders and looked at Mike. Mike Rignelli shrugged his shoulders and screamed,

"Play Ball!"

The Simmons family won the toss and took the ball out first. Dennis was still nervous because of the way he was introduced. As soon as the game began Dennis went into college mode. He made sure he passed the ball to all of the family member s equally. His mission wasn't just to win, but to win fairly and make a good impression on the family.

The Simmons family curse was broken. Dennis ended the game with a slam dunk. Directly after the game was over, Mike jokingly said to Phillip,

"Admit it, Ole Dennis there, is a ringer."

"Let's eat" Phillip replied.

Dennis and Jackie noticed quite a bit of stares and whisperers. Jackie's mother was quiet and remained distracted to avoid the elephant in the room.

This was the first time Dennis had eaten pumpkin pie. Dennis had built up in his mind before arriving for this big 'shocked' reaction from the Simmons family. But they weren't shocked. They didn't ask a bunch of questions. Quite the contrary, they spoke around him as if he was invisible. They were more comfortable with Dennis than Dennis was with them

Dennis thought this could be good or bad. Either he wasn't a big deal, or he was. Jackie and Dennis collected all of the equipment and took it with them when they left a tad bit early. Jackie was in charge of the equipment. It was always kept at her place. Phillip and Mike were responsible for the food and beverages. Jackie's mom Linda was in charge of location. Mike's wife Gloria Rignelli was responsible for the uniforms.

The uniforms were usually colored T-Shirts. Dennis dropped Jackie off at home and thanked her for a wonderful time. Dennis had also packed two plates. One for his mother and one for himself for later. Dennis went to his mom's house without Jackie on purpose. He wanted to talk to his mother without reservations. He knew his mother would sensor her conversation if he brought Jackie.

It was Saturday and Dennis looked forward to Saturday morning breakfast with his mother. He had told her Thursday that he would be there after 6pm for dinner because of the game. Florence felt that would be fine. That gave her time in the morning to run errands. She loved going shopping with Catherine and Princess from department store to department store.

I'm Leaving You For A White Woman

When Dennis pulled up, he saw Catherine's car out front. This time he didn't wait in the car. This time he went straight in using the key. Catherine said hello and handed Dennis another summons. Dennis put it in his back pocket without looking at it. Dennis always tried his best to be calm and in control of his anger in front of his mother and Princess.

Dennis placed the plates on the table. Catherine left but Princess stayed. Catherine took away two weekends a month from Dennis only to give them to his mother. That whole thing left an ugly taste in his mouth. It made him feel as if his mother was on the side of the person who brings him pain. That thought caused him as much pain as the pain itself.

Dennis and Princess shared one plate and Florence ate the other one. Florence complained about the meat but cleaned her plate. Dennis thought nothing of it because his mother always complained about meals she didn't cook. No restaurant was exempt from her criticism.

"Are you serious about that white girl or are you just going through a phase?"

"Jackie's my girlfriend if that s what you're asking" Dennis defensively responded.

Dennis had anticipated such a response. He had rehearsed answers to questions he knew he would be asked. He knew from the hospital silence that they'd be vocal later.

159

His mother never approved of any women he dated so he knew Jackie would be no different. Dennis wasn't surprised. Only the simple minded would have issues with someone they've never met.

Over the years following the death of his father, Dennis love for is mother grew. But the respect he once felt for her had diminished a great deal. Over the years he became more protective of her since she lived alone.

"How long have y'all been dating?"

"Three weeks to a month. I mean we just clicked."

"Y'all couldn't have nothing in common."

"Well, me and Catherine had a lot in common and look what happened."

The word was out now. Dennis was sure he and Jackie were the topic of discussion for the entire weened after leaving the hospital. Dennis was also carful how he answered Florence's questions. He knew whatever he told his mother, Catherine would hear later. He was also conscious of the fact that Princess was on the couch watching cartoons.

Princess was respectfully pretending not to listen. But Dennis knew his daughter well. She was studious and inquisitive. Florence told Dennis that she and Daphne talked about it most of the night. She had never known him to date outside his race before. She had the 'whatever makes you happy' attitude, but Daphne took a more hard-lined approach.

Aunt Daphne was texting some ugly racist comments to their shared constituency. Dennis pulled the summons from his back pocket and read it. Catherine was attempting to limit his visits to supervised visits only. The summons was baseless. Because his arrests were violent in nature, there was a good chance that Catherine's request would be granted.

Dennis asked his mother did she know about the summons. She swore to him she didn't. When Dennis asked for advice, she told hm that she didn't want to get involved. Since when? Dennis thought to himself. He didn't remember a time when she wasn't involved. She would strategically place herself in the middle only to express her discontent for it.

Dennis gave Princess a long hug then went home. The date and time were set for Monday at 8:30am. Dennis went straight in and called Jackie. During the recap of today's events and excitement, Dennis didn't know whether to mention his Monday court appointment to her. Everything was going perfectly, and the last thing Dennis wanted to do was spoil it. He didn't want to bring his old problems into his new relationship. He wanted to give Jackie a chance with a man with no issues.

He felt Catherine's drama was his problem, not hers. He feared losing her behind what he referred to as 'Negro shit.' Which meant small, petty, personal problems with dire consequences. Dennis was fed up with 'Nigro shit' and its extreme collateral damage. He found himself the victim of attacks with nothing to gain but by the attacker. Dennis began to notice how Negro shit had ruined his life unprovoked.

He was falsely accused of domestic violence and placed in jail. After he got out of jail, he had to endure 52 weeks of court ordered classes. He fell in love with a woman he thought loved him. Only to find her with a man sexually she just met. Dennis had the phrase "Nice guys finish last" manifest itself in physical form. After receiving a beating from Derek, he went back to jail again. This time it cost him his job.

Dennis couldn't ever find the problem because he was looking for one distinct person or event. Because there wasn't one. He began to realize it was an atmosphere the black women in his life represented. The entire atmosphere is what he was done with. That never-ending tennis match of monotonous pain. The atmosphere of unhappiness of people who find delight in the pain of others. They're so immersed in the pain that they actually referred to their lives as "The Struggle."

In constant pursue of the next negative news to gossip about. The crab in the barrel mentality. He began to recognize the emasculation campaign by black women even within his own family. He began to develop an anger in himself. He no longer felt trapped by his circumstances, his surroundings, and his simple-minded relatives anymore.

Dennis had become so obsessed with finding a black woman and making it work to the point where he could not recognize his own abuse nor abusers. That sassy, feisty, diva, neck rolling, loud, rude behavior that the black women in his life seemed to take so much pride in. This "strong black woman" tag which displayed ignorance rather than strength.

Dennis loved his mother, aunt and sister. This very love had festered over the years as a duty to the point of Dennis developing a self-perpetuated Stockholm syndrome. Dennis was willing to put up with anything to protect what he viewed as his family structure. Now he felt like a victim of a mirage.

As Jackie and he spoke, he felt as if he had been given and out where there wasn't one previously. He remembered being with the Simmons family. There was no gossip, negative conversations nor fights, just fun. Sometimes a person gets sick and tired of feeling sick and tired. He and Jackie would discuss taking it slow. Then sometimes they'd talk about taking it to the next level. Two hurt people who decided to heal each other.

Dennis was afraid to lay it all out there too soon. He got off the phone with Jackie. He called Bob to tell him he wouldn't be at work Monday and why. Since this was the first day off he'd requested, Bob didn't mind. Dennis made 500 per week. 100 dollars a day cash. There was no pay on days he didn't work. Unlike when he was teaching.

About twice a month Dennis would call Bill Toliver. Just to stay in touch. Dennis called Jackie back and her phone went straight to voicemail. As soon as he put his phone down it rang. It was

Jackie. They both laughed about the fact they were both calling each other at the same time. Jackie did all she could to talk Dennis into letting her come over to spend the night. Jackie had gotten to the point where she no longer wanted to sleep alone. Dennis had developed a severe case of P.T.S.D. from his traumatic experiences with black women. He knew if he was too cautious, he may lose her.

Jackie was scared also but her fear manifested itself optimistically. Dennis loved talking to Jackie all night. They both enjoyed falling asleep on the phone together. Jackie was a Scorpio with a naivest interest in astrology. Dennis was a libra, always playing it safe.

Dennis told Jackie he was about to go to sleep. Jackie replied, "Too late, I just pulled up. I'm out front." Dennis smiled as he walked over to the front door to unlock it. Jackie asked where his daughter was. Dennis explained the situation to her.

Jackie was determined to go to court with Dennis. She wanted to show her support and she wasn't taking no for an answer. Dennis agreed but with a reluctant heart. Jackie was careful with her words. Since she didn't have children of her own, she could only sympathize, not empathize. Daphne had Catherine all fired up.

"What game is Dennis playing?" asked Catherine.

"I know girl. Showing up in the hospital with that white girl. That's how you know he's not over you yet. Cuz he's still trying to hurt you and get yo attention."

I'm Leaving You For A White Woman

"I know. I don't care about that white bitch."

"He must hate his momma. I can't believe my nephew is a sell-out."

"No, what it is Daphne…. What it is you know he just can't handle a strong black woman. These brothas go get these white bitches because they do whatever they say!" exclaimed Catherine.

Daphne spent the night throwing coals on the fire of fury that Catherine had ignited. For some reason, Daphne and Catherine equated Dennis being with Jackie as if he was rejecting all black women/people everywhere. Daphne and Catherine fed off each other's deep seeded bitterness until they created an unnecessary monster.

Catherine mainly got her relationship advice from Florence, a divorcee and Daphne, who had never been married. Those simple facts seemed illogical to Dennis. To Dennis it made no logical sense. Daphne was Dennis' favorite aunt. Florence loved her son Dennis. But Catherine held a mysterious allure when it came to Daphne and Florence.

Catherine hated to see Dennis happy or enjoying a fraction of success. Dennis somehow knew his newfound happiness would stir up ugly thoughts and evil actions from women close to him. Women who claimed to love him. Even though Catherine knew any success Dennis had would mean more success for Princess. That fact was of no importance to Catherine who was so blinded by hate she couldn't see clearly.

It became clear to Dennis that she hated him more than she loved Princess. The entire night before court, Dennis spoke to Jackie. He personally felt that their relationship was too early for such vulnerability. But once Dennis opened the can of worms, she couldn't close it.

Jackie could hear the painful desperation in Dennis's voice. In all of Jackie's previous relationships, no man has ever been so open and honest with her. She wasn't sure of what she was feeling. Whatever it was, she liked it. His emotional outcry touched her in a way that nothing else had. The more he spoke, the deeper she felt.

That night Dennis and Jackie didn't break the ice, they melted it. They spoke all night into the morning. Dennis hadn't ever known love so tender and gentile. The women in his life were like sandpaper, hard, coarse and aggressive. They tried so hard to be strong (or what they viewed as strength) they forgot how to properly give and receive unconditional love along the way.

Dennis' heart was in Jackie's hands. Jackie expressed to Dennis that he was like no man she'd ever been with. A warm man who's not afraid to be vulnerable. She saw his total honesty as strength. Jackie was overjoyed, alas, a real man in her life. Strong and tender. He was as thoughtful as he was thought provoking.

In her past she'd been weak for the tall blonde surfer types. She had been misused by the good looking and patronized by the corporate type.

I'm Leaving You For A White Woman

Jackie just wanted to matter to someone. And she mattered to Dennis. Jackie saw Dennis as smart, strong, sensitive and wise. She was attracted to his intellect.

Dennis felt whole with Jackie. He could feel her respect whenever he spoke. The black women in Dennis' life weren't attracted to qualities he possessed. He felt valued and appreciated for the first time by any woman.

Dennis tried his best to make a family with Catherine. But Catherine grew up with just her mother. The men in her family weren't noteworthy to say the least. It was the women in her family who made the money and took care of the men like overgrown children. So, she grew up not expecting much from them which brewed into a lack of respect for black men in general.

A subconscious disdain if you will. When Dennis would exercise his masculinity, Catherine would take offense to it personally. Since the women in her world had to be both mothers and fathers. So, whenever Dennis preformed a fatherly duty, Catherine saw it as "stepping on her toes."

His paternal instincts held no respect when viewed alongside to her maternal instincts. To Catherine, men were only needed for conception. Catherine, and black women like Catherine have reduced the black man's worth to a body part and or a paycheck. This was a dangerous practice with devastating consequences.

In doing this, they unknowingly transformed themselves into Black Widow spiders. In the insect community, the Black Widow spider is a female who'd kill and eat her male counterpart once they became pregnant. Many black men have gotten the message and heeded warning. For those black men in the graveyard and others in the penitentiary, it's too little too late.

Men and women are symbionically connected like a seesaw. What effects one instantly effects the other. By condensing the black man's worth to a paycheck, the black woman unwittingly reduces her own self-worth to a body part, her ass. Her ass has become the criteria she used to rate herself along with her outward appearance.

Parenting to Catherine was a one-woman job. Dennis was so tired and completely through with the weave wearing neck rollers. He was raised in a respectable two parent home. His parents were married many years before he and his sister were born. They operated as a unit until the separation and the divorce that followed.

Jackie opened up to Dennis about herself like no other. She expresses that she's been an eclectic, optimistic extrovert all her life. That she didn't get good grades in school and was deemed a social misfit because if it. She had a 'surfer hippie' type of style with cheerleader looks. Dennis was exactly the opposite.

Dennis was an intellectual introvert. He was deemed a social misfit because he got good grades. However, while Dennis spent his post high school days on the basketball court and college campus. Often ridiculed by other guys for wearing his heart on his sleeve.

Chapter 10

The next morning Dennis work up with a
troubled mind. He dressed in a suit suitable for
court, had a cup of coffee, then left with Jackie.
Jackie went to the restroom while Dennis walked in
the courtroom alone. Catherine was already there
alone. She assumed Dennis was alone too. They
both made eye contact but kept a suitable distance
from one another.

Just as their names were called, Jackie
walked in. Jackie sat in the seat that Dennis got up
from. He handed her his coat. As much as Dennis
told her he didn't want her to attend, he was happy
she was there. To Dennis, it made all the difference
in the world when Jackie walked in to show her
support. Jackie remembered how she felt when
Dennis stepped out on the basketball court. How he
didn't want to because of the bittersweet memories
of almost making it to the NBA but he did it

anyway to support her. When he did, she felt as though her hero had arrived to lead the Simmons family to victory, breaking the 4-year curse.

Catherine began presenting her case. Dennis didn't know why he was in court or what was Catherine's motivation. Catherine had copies of Dennis arrest record for the assault on Byron and restraining order filed by La Ronda. That information she could have only gotten from Florence. Only certain people knew he had been arrested and lost his teaching job.

The judge began to speak and was cut off by one of Catherine's rants. Catherine went on an emotional rant and demanded that Dennis be given supervised visits.

"On what basis?" asked the judge.

"He is violent, he has no job, but he has money to date white bitches. I don't know what kind of people he's bringing my daughter around."

The courtroom gasped several times during her rant then fell upon a dead silence following the "White Bitch" comment.

"Do you provide Mr. Alexander a list of men you date and their sources of income?" asked the judge.

"I'm her mother, I don't have to." The judge looked at Dennis and shook his head. He himself couldn't believe her twisted narcistic logic. The judge asked Dennis about his income. Since he was still paying

600 a month still in child support, he told the judge.
Dennis told the judge that he'd been working as a
landscaper and sometimes day laborer. He told the
judge he made 500 dollars a week.

First the judge lowered his child support to
300 dollars a month. The judge correctly reset the
child support based on Dennis's income. The judge
explained that he wouldn't reduce any of Dennis
time. He granted Dennis every weekend back like
before, with one stipulation. The judge ordered
Dennis to make known to Catherine if or when his
occupation or income changes. Dennis agreed.

Dennis was successful in court. He didn't
want Jackie to know that he wasn't teaching. That
he was basically cutting lawns for a living. Even
though he won, he walked out of court with his
head hanging low. Jackie ran up behind him just as
the double doors were closing and hugged him from
behind. She kissed him on the back of the neck in
plain view of Catherine.

Catherine silently rolled her eyes and began
feverishly pressing the elevator button. Just then,
Dennis spun around and gave Jackie the biggest hug
and kiss as if he had just come back from The War.
When the elevator came, Catherine quickly got in it.
Dennis and Jackie decided to take the next one.
Dennis felt better instantly. Apparently, the judge
saw through Catherine's vindictive fury.

Dennis knew she'd be going straight to his
mom's house. But he didn't care. He was happier
than he had been in a while. Jackie offered to treat
Dennis to lunch. They drove to her favorite Tai

restaurant. As always, they enjoyed each other's company.

"How come you told me you were a teacher?"

"Because I am. Just not currently" answered Dennis.

"Tomato, tomato Dennis. It doesn't matter to me one way or the other." Explained Jackie.

"I wasn't ashamed of my landscaping job. I was ashamed at how I lost my teaching job" said Dennis.

He was ashamed he had gone to jail and was still going to court over the incident. Dennis loved Tai food. Jackie had no way of knowing this. This was just one more thing the two of them had in common. They both ate and laughed about today's events. This was one of the hurdles Dennis felt he had to jump over. His next fight would be avoiding any more jail time in his assault case.

He would still be eligible to work as a teacher come next Fall. But if he loses his assault case and actually goes to prison, then he would be permanently barred from teaching. Dennis took Jackie home. She had also missed a day of work, so she had double the number of clients tomorrow. She had asked Dennis to say a while. She knew he couldn't spend the night. He had to be at work at 5am. But it was still early.

Dennis agreed to stay just a few hours. Jackie made Dennis a tuna casserole. Well, she

attempted to make. While they were both eating, Jackie asked him,
"What do you think?"

"It's delicious!"

"Yep, you'll make a good husband."

"Why do you say that?"

"Cause, you already know when to lie."

They both kept a straight face until they both just laughed. Dennis left as expected a few hours after arriving.

He decided to stop by Dana's house. Tasha had been calling him for days. He had planned on stopping by Tasha's house some time that week. He missed spending time with his pal. Dennis hadn't seen or even really spoked to his sister Dana since the whole Byron, La Ronda incident.

Dana wasn't overjoyed to see Dennis to say the least. She also felt Dennis owed Derek an apology. The only person Dennis felt he owed an apology to was Jasmine. And Dennis was the last person on Earth Jasmin ever wanted to see again.

Dana was angry and disappointed with Dennis, but she wasn't angry. Dennis was and will always be her baby brother. Dana was worried how Derek would react when he saw Dennis. Dennis wasn't worried because he remembers Derek smiling at him in the hospital.

As soon as Derek walked in and saw Dennis his face lit up. He came in with an extra-large super deluxe pizza and a container of hot wings. "Stay and join us brother-in-law" Derek said to Dennis. Even though Dana and Derek weren't legally married they'd been together so long that the family treated them like they were. Since Derek didn't mention Byron, Dennis chose not to bring him up either. "Naw man, I've been eating all day. Well, a slice won't kill me."

Dana and Derek spent their evenings sitting on the couch watching sports. This evening would be no different. Dennis expected for Dana and Derek to ask him about court. But instead, Derek came and blind-sided Dennis with, "Hey, who was that fine ass white girl at the hospital with you?" When the phrase "fine ass white girl" left Derek's lips Dana popped him on the back of his head. Derek shrugged his shoulders and whispered to Dana, "What I say?"

Dennis by now had gotten use to saying, 'She's my girlfriend.' But he wasn't still use to the shocked and surprised looks his response generated. Dana pretended as if the game on television was more interesting than what Dennis and Derek were about to discuss. Derek asked Dennis where did she and Jackie meet?

Dennis knew that was a 'gal' question, not a 'guy' question. He could tell by the way it was asked that it originated form Dana, not Derek. By that he knew they had been discussing him and Jackie. He also knew that this would be just one question in a series of questions. Dennis smiled

because these questions he could easily handle. He
was afraid Derek would bring up La Ronda or even
Byron. Dennis didn't know Derek's relationship
with Byron. They could be brothers, cousins,
friends or just co-workers
    "We met at a pizza parlor" replied Dennis.
Dennis kept his answers short and to the point. He
knew an interview when he heard one.

"Which pizza parlor?" asked Derek.

"Why you wanna know?" Dana interrupted. Dennis
stated laughing and answered to give Derek an out.

"Just know that I'm very happy in my relationship."

Dennis directed his answer at the both of them. "As
long as you're happy" said Derek.
    Dennis excused himself. He knew he had to
be at work early the next morning. On his way
home he called Bill Toliver. Bill stated that he's still
working on something with Dennis in mind. Right
now, it was still in the air. But prospects looked
promising. To Dennis that was great news.
    When Dennis got home, he called Tasha.
She had called to ask him about Jackie, apparently.
Dennis wondered if Jackie was getting bombarded
with questions and assumptions by the people in her
life as he was. Dennis noticed a condescending
accusatory tone to her questions and voice.
    Dennis first assumed that Tasha may be just
a little jealous because another woman was
interfering with their talk time. But Dennis never

expected that Tasha would take it so personally. Especially since the two never dated. Tasha was pissed when she heard about Jackie.

She first accused Dennis of being with Jackie for prestige like a status symbol. As if she was some sort of trophy. Dennis fired back stating that Tasha assumed that Jackie was the prize, and not Dennis. As far as Dennis was concerned, being with a white woman in no way changed American society's opinions of black men. Then Tasha assumed that Jackie or her family had money. Dennis told Tasha that Jackie was a massage therapist and that they are both in the same tax bracket. Then Tasha accused Dennis of wanting to make pretty mixed babies with Jackie. As if a black baby born of black parents can't be pretty.

That's the one that really irked Dennis. Dennis was so shocked by Tasha's tirade. She was a mother to a mixed child. Besides that, she only dated White men, Asian men or mixed, high yellow black men. So far Tasha was his worst critic. Dennis found himself justifying his feelings towards Jackie. It was beginning to slightly anger him, though he didn't let on.

Tasha accused him of wanting to hurt his mother. She had implied any black man with a white woman must not love his mother. Dennis told Tasha then a black woman with a white man hates her father. He had flipped it around to show her its absurdity. Dennis also stated that "A compliment to one woman isn't an insult to another. To say I like my aunt's car doesn't mean I hate my mother's car."

I'm Leaving You For A White Woman

Tasha accused his recent switch as a rejection of his mom. Dennis told her if he were to date a woman like his mom in every way would mean he's sexually attracted to his mother. Dennis told Tasha how sick that would be.

"My father and I don't have the same taste in women. Florence is my father's woman, not mines. Are you telling me I should be attracted to women who look and act like my mom? That sounds like some sick, Oedipus, Norman Bates type stuff. Or are you saying that black women are so insecure that every man must find them physically attractive including white men and all black men including their sons?" asked Dennis.

He felt Tasha was being unfairly hypocritical. Dennis thought for sure he had Tasha's vote. The way Dennis saw it, if he chooses a woman as a mate who was just like his mother it would mean he had some sick Oedipus complex. To him that made no sense at all.

But then Dennis remembered how Tasha would refer to every light-skinned male as fine, but she would tare down light-skinned women. He realized Tasha was jealous and deep down wished her own complexion was lighter. She envied the straight hair and complexion of light-skinned women so much that she tried as much as she could to mimic their look.

Dennis began to notice her mandatory weaves, how her make-up was lighter than her own complexion. Dennis was extremely disappointed in Tasha. "Black men don't find me attractive" said

Tasha. "Yes, we do. But you don't feel attractive unless white men find you attractive. Stop saying society doesn't like dark-skinned women. That's a lie. Black men are a part of society and we find you attractive. But you don't respect us nor our opinion. You don't care if we find you attractive as long as White men do. You're the one who talks that good-hair stuff. You hated La Ronda because she was mixed but you wish to have a child who looks like her. Truth is, you wished you looked like her, don't you!"

To him she sounded like a confused racist. It seemed to Dennis that Tasha hated black men and white women. But she loved white men. Every time Dennis pointed out a character flaw in the majority of black women he'd come in contact with her response "So!" She justified every mistake she or any black woman ever made. If she didn't respond with "so," then somehow it was black men's fault. Everything was "Strong black women" this or "Strong black women" that.

Dennis cut Tasha off in mid-sentence;

"Tasha, you are as black as the Ace of Spade and you wear a 30-inch platinum blonde weave."

"Fuck you Dennis, you black too" she replied.

"Unlike you, I consider it a compliment, not an insult."

Dennis threw the blonde weave comment in as an insult. But Tasha didn't consider the blonde weave comment as in insult. Instead she was insulted by the "Ace of Spade" comment. The 'Ace of Spade' comment was an observation, not an insult. Tasha didn't hate her race, she hated her complexion. She saw dark skin as a curse. The more Dennis spoke to Tasha, the more respect he lost for her. But this conversation/argument was a long-time coming. Dennis felt sorry for her son. She refused to cut his hair because like she said, "He has good hair, it isn't nappy." So she kept his hair in a ponytail like a girl all of the time. What information was she going to raise him with?

The conversation with Tasha was wearing him out. Usually he just agreed to disagree when it came to her. But it was different this time. This time he felt she was attacking Jackie. He had grown defensive when he felt someone was attacking the woman he was falling in love with.

When Dennis met Jackie's father Phillip, he assumed he'd hit the floor. Dennis had assumed the racism and ugliness would come from her family. But to his disappointment, it was coming from his side. And Tasha of all people. He pretty much got the message from his family (at least the women) that Jackie wasn't welcomed.

Dennis saw this as their loss. Jackie was a fun, funny, quick-witted, insightful, compassionate and gentile woman, but all they could see was White. They felt that Dennis was insulting them personally. His particular choice had nothing to do with them.

When Dennis got off the phone, he called Jackie to clear his head. Dennis was hoping Tasha

wasn't mad at him. He loved Tasha but he didn't
see her in the same light anymore. But she was his
best friend and entitled to her opinion. While
Dennis was talking to Jackie, he texted Tasha a
heart and a happy face. That was his way of
showing that there were no hard feelings between
them. Tasha didn't text him back

Jackie had asked could she spend the night
with Dennis. Dennis told her sure. They both had
copies of each other's house keys. Dennis told
Jackie to just use her key in the likelihood he's
asleep. Jackie and Dennis were growing
comfortable with one another. They had passed the
stage where they felt they had to display each other.
The two were irresistibly drawn to each other.
Dennis found himself spending half his weeks at
Jackie's house. The other half, Jackie spent at his
house.

Dennis had become spoiled with a full body
massage every night from a licensed professional.
Jackie felt safe in Dennis' arms. It was becoming
harder and harder for Jackie to leave and return
home to sleep alone. But the interracial aspect
remained providing an allure that felt forbidden.
They were each other's best sexual experience as
well as first interracial relationship.

The two of them had yet to bring up race to
each other. They didn't treat it as an elephant in the
room. To the two of them it wasn't an issue worth
mentioning. Dennis wasn't sure if it was him or just
everyone else. Both Dennis and Jackie were adults.
Sometimes when they were together on a date, both

would notice certain looks, stares and under the breath comments. Surprising to Dennis, most of the evil looks and under the breath comments came from blacks, not whites. Primarily black women. He had assumed it would be from white men. They just ignored them. The looks mostly came from white men and comments from black women. While lying in the bed spooning, Dennis asked,

"What does your father and mother say to you about our relationship?" The answer Jackie gave blew his mind.

"Nothing, I'm a grown woman, I mean I'm 28 years old. How pathetic would it be if they had any opinion at all?"

Dennis was taken back. He had assumed all families were nosey, opinionated and judgmental like his. Then to lighten the mood Jackie said,

"Oh, my father did say that no matter what happens to our relationship, you're invited to our basketball games permanently."

Then they both laughed. Tasha had been and will always be an important part of Dennis's life. Thus, making her family. Being that, this gave Tasha certain privileges with Dennis that his other friends didn't have.

People found Dennis it odd that he didn't
have a pack of male friends or "His boys." His best
friend was a woman who would do anything for
him but spent most of her time debating or arguing
with him. Whenever Tasha needed Dennis he would
be there without question. Tasha's son Jason calls
him Uncle Dennis.

Tasha had called Dennis' mother to get the
latest gossip. Florence had expressed on many
occasions that if Dennis didn't marry Catherine then
she would want Tasha as her daughter in-law. No
matter how many times Dennis told his mother that
he and Tasha were just close friends it never sunk
in. Tasha was just as much Florence's friend as she
was Dennis'.

Tasha couldn't stand Catherine. She saw
Catherine as a vindictive leach. She felt Catherine
only came around when she wanted something.
Tasha was also a tad bit jealous because she didn't
have any type of consistent help at all with her child
like Catherine did. Florence had no gossip to give
Tasha. Florence said that she didn't know what had
gotten into her son. Florence referred to Jackie as
"That white girl."

After losing in court, Catherine had not been
by Florence's house with the baby. Florence had a
good conversation with Tasha. Daphne and Tasha
spoke every day. When Tasha needed advice, she
called Florence. When Tasha wanted to hit a bar
and grill, she called Daphne. Tasha hadn't spoken to
her own mother in over a year. No particular reason,
her family just wasn't that close.

I'm Leaving You For A White Woman

Through the entire week, Jackie stayed at Dennis's house. The two of them were kind of on a trial run. For the entire week they woke up together, showered together, cooked for one another, etc. Since the new court ruling, this was the first weekend of many to come that Dennis could have Princess. He was experiencing a great deal of anxiety as the week came to a close.

He had to pick up Princess Friday and he had his final session with the therapist. Thursday night the butterflies were loose in his stomach. Bill Toliver had been keeping in touch with updates. Most of the usual people in Dennis's life were becoming scarce.

They were noticing a developmental change in him. He was running out of patience for what he once had patience for. Jackie had met Princess once at the pizza parlor. But she had not been formally introduced as Jackie, her father's new girlfriend. Dennis and Jackie shared a common bond through laughter and a sense of freedom.

Jackie brought a Zen quality that fit well with his beta-masculine demeanor. But Jackie didn't physically fit the profile of a Zen-type tree hugger. Jackie looked more like an Amber or a Heather. She stood 5'10". She was what white men refer to as a bombshell. Long Marsha Brady blonde hair with an athletic body. Since Dennis wasn't initially attracted to white girls, he didn't recognize her as stacked. Thus, he wasn't intimidated by her as most men were.

Since he wasn't distracted by her flawless appearance, he was able to speak directly to her inner self. This turned Jackie on. She had finally met a man who was attracted to her heart and not what she looked like or represented. To Jackie, the fact that Dennis didn't care or commented how beautiful she was on the outside and only showed her how beautiful she was on the inside, mattered most.

Dennis was no 'Joe Schmo' himself. He also held an impressive outward appearance with an athletic build himself. He was well groomed and well educated. Though his current tax bracket may disagree. He was never the guy who sought out to impress woman. He had "No game" to say the least. But the black women Dennis dated were turned off by his "lack of game". They were too silly, immature and narrowminded to understand that men with "game" play games.

A real man need not those things to serve as distractions. A real man needs only to present himself open and honestly. This was Dennis's first experience with a true counterpart. Jackie was a woman as open and honest as he was. Friday came as it always does at the end of the work week. But this particular Friday came after much anticipation. Dennis had an average day at work, grueling and back breaking. But this Friday he knew he'd be going home to a massage. He also had his last one on one evaluation session, and he'd be formally introducing Princess to Jackie.

Dennis also had a future court day looming over his head. Dennis was no street kid. He was a college man and he carried himself as such. He wasn't nervous, he was scared. The thought of going to prison terrified him. He was well aware of the repercussions and collateral damage it would cause. The effects would be felt as far down the line as Princess.

He knew he'd need to hire a lawyer. But with landscaping as his only source of income, a lawyer wasn't in the budget. These thoughts took an immediate back seat as he got closer to his appointment. He had no idea what to expect.

For the entire day, he kept replaying what Jackie said to him in bed over and over in his head. 'How pathetic would it be if her parents had any opinion at all?' Her parents trust her decisions, because they knew who and what they'd raised. The way Dennis saw it; If his mother didn't trust his decisions and she raised him, then she was actuality doubting herself.

Chapter 11

Dennis walked into his appointment as
usual. He laid back in his usual position on the
therapist' couch. The therapist said, "Dennis you
suffer from Gynophobia. Caused by the P.T.S.D.
(Post-Traumatic Stress Disorder) starting with the
death of your father. That which stimmed into
misdirected pain.

Since there wasn't a suitable outlet provided
for you, the pain turned inward and festered into
guilt. The guilt you carried as an unfulfilled labor of
love. You felt your mother was cheated. Thus,
leaving a huge hole inside of her. No amount of bar-
b-que ribs, Princess visits, money or gossip can fill
it. Sometimes even with a hole were complete.
Like a doughnut or a tire.

You set out to be the man every woman in
your life needed. That's why it never seemed
enough. You're so many things to so many women
at the end you ended up nothing to no one. Not even

to yourself. You, and men like you have been abused to the point of Stockholm syndrome. You've allowed yourself, the victim, to be victimized again and again because you feel you deserve it.

The women in your life have convinced you that they are as good as you'll get and all you deserve and or worth. Once you bought into this belief, you began seeking to settle. Thus, permanently perpetuating your own pain into a private hell. You're not a criminal but you now have a criminal record. Every ounce of pain you've ever experienced came from the women you selected to surround yourself with.

Women have cost you your freedom, your job, your money, self-respect, time with your daughter you can't get back. Look at yourself, honestly. You're in a relationship specialist office for a relationship you're no longer in but still suffer devastating effects from. You blamed your mother for your father's departure, not his death.

If I can recall, your parents were separated and divorced at the time of his death. Just the mere loss of the primary economic provider thrusted you, your sister and your mother into a position of adapting to a lifestyle you were not accustomed to. The fact that you haven't gone completely bonkers and killed all of these people is a miracle in and of itself.

You live in a hell that I myself couldn't conceive of functioning in. Remember, at the end of the day, the person who matters most is the one who lives in the mirror."

I'm Leaving You For A White Woman

Dennis took it all in, and for the first time in his life, everything was as clear as the first day of summer. He felt new, born again, free. His veil of despair and self-pity had been lifted. "I can't thank you enough. I owe you my life" said Dennis. The therapist smiled and said "No Dennis, that's what you owe yourself. My fee is pre-paid."

Dennis hadn't called Jackie all day. Usually they spoke once a day at his lunch break. Dennis was hoping she was still at his place. He drove straight to pick up Princess. His happiness was radiantly glowing and all who crossed his path could see it, feel it.

Catherine could no longer upset him. His family could not use guilt to control him. When Princess and Dennis walked in to see Jackie, Princess screamed "The Pizza Lady!" Dennis was glad she remembered. It made the next part, the reintroduction, a little easier.

The End.

AFTERMATH

Dennis and Jackie both moved in together into Dennis' apartment to save money. They soon were married afterwards, saved their money and bought a house together in the suburbs as Mr. and Mrs. Alexander. Far away from Dennis' family. Dennis got the job at the Jr. high school in the area as the assistant Dean. That new master's degree came in handy. He was hired personally by Bill Toliver, the new principle. Dennis was given 3 years summary probation for the La Ronda incident.

Jackie loved the new house. Just 15 minutes from her job. When Dennis moved, he redefined his relationship with his family to holidays only. Dennis distanced himself from Tasha. He had outgrown his former self and his newly cleansed soul/spirit left no room for negativity of any kind.

Within a year into Dennis and Jackie's marriage they welcomed the arrival of a baby boy named Phoenix (Rise from the ashes) Alexander. Dennis still coach's basketball. In the pee-wee league, ages 10-12 at the local park.

For the first time in the life of Dennis Alexander he knows true happiness.

Other Books by Mickey Royal currently available on Amazon.com and mickeyroyal.com

The Pimp Game: Instructional Guide...........14.95

The former Hollywood king reveals secret techniques with proven results on mastering the art of submission. A look inside the mind of the master as well as a chilling peek into the shadow world. A modern-day guide parallel to The Prince by Machiavelli.

Along For The Ride...........14.95

An autobiographical account of how Mickey Royal establishes The Royal Family; an organized stable of prostitutes, which runs with the efficiency of a Fortune 500 company. At the same time, this powerful family takes on crooked cops, overzealous music executives, drug lords and the Muslim Mafia to solve a six-year-old murder mystery.

Pimping Ain't Easy:
But Somebody's Gotta Do It.................14.95

Coffee, a journalism student on spring break who has been given the assignment of a lifetime. She follows Mickey Royal around for seven days as she gathers intel for her mid-term. She soon finds herself entangled in the shadow world and embarks on an adventure she won't soon forget.

191

Other Books by Mickey Royal currently available on Amazon.com and mickeyroyal.com

I'm Leaving you for a White Woman..........14.95

Dennis, seeing no other way to solve the problems in his relationship seeks the counseling of a therapist. During his soul-searching excavation, he un-earths repressed feelings of emasculation and anxiety, due to decades of systematic subliminally subconscious emotional abuse at the hands of Black Women. Painstakingly arriving to the conclusion that many Black Men have. But until now, were afraid to come forward.

The Pimp Game: Secrets of Mind Manipulation 14.95

From the author of The Pimp Game: Instructional Guide comes Book 2, advanced lessons in psychological mastery. Techniques of secret societies which dissect and explain how so few minds control so many. What makes one submit to the will of another?

About the author

Mickey Royal resides in Los Angeles where he is currently writing his next book. Contact him on Facebook or at mickeyroyal.com
Email; mickeyroyal2016@yahoo.com

I'm Leaving You For A White Woman

Made in the USA
Monee, IL
17 June 2020

33803520R00108